Mary Brunton
The Forgotten Scottish Novelist

Mary Brunton
The Forgotten Scottish Novelist

Mary McKerrow

The Orcadian Limited

Printed and Published by The Orcadian Limited,
Hell's Half Acre, Hatston, Kirkwall, Orkney, KW15 1DW.
Tel. 01856 879000. Fax 01856 879001

All rights reserved © The Estate of Mary McKerrow

ISBN 1-902957-05-9

Published 2001

The contents of this book may not be reproduced in any form without written permission of the publishers, except for short extracts for quotation or review.

For Alison

Contents

List of Illustrations

Foreword

Mary McKerrow, author of this delightful book, and much to my shame, died at the age of 85 before I had finished and delivered this foreword. It is because of scholars and enthusiasts of the kind Mary McKerrow so typifies, and of publishers like *The Orcadian*, that the literature of the past is not forgotten, but continues to be a source of pleasure and intelligence to those of a bookish kind: it ill behoves a still living writer to put these things off. Better to pay attention at once.

But Mary McKerrow did at least have the satisfaction of knowing her book was to be published, that so much compelling research, so great a degree of dedicated biographical endeavour, was to bear fruit. She was aware of the lasting contribution to the annals she was about to make. And by any standards this is a significant book, a pleasure to read, and a fascinating of how 'if you're born to write, write you will write.' Who would have thought that plain Mary Balfour, born in Durham but bred in far Orkney, would become Mary Brunton, best selling novelist, rival in her time to Jane Austen, and a leading light in Edinburgh's then flourishing and sophisticated literary circles. As with Jane Austen, Mary Brunton's talent seemed to spring out of nowhere, and as with Jane Austen, her life was not to be long. Both had only some forty years in which to make their mark on the world. Both wrote at a time when for a woman to be a writer was not seen as the desirable thing it is now, but carried with it a degree of social opprobrium. For a woman's fancy to roam outside marriage and the home was not the thing. Even the reading of novels was seen as frivolous, and inflaming to the delicate imagination. Very, very far from the days of Eng.Lit. as taught in our schools today.

The very titles of Mary Brunton's two popular novels, *Self Control* (1811) and *Discipline* (1814) suggest that they are part of her attempt to be thought virtuous – she was after all married to a clergyman – though she had in the first place eloped with him, and in the most dramatic manner, to escape the opposition of her military family. She did not lack courage, either in her writing or her life, but was just very well aware of the social responsibility of the writer.

It is interesting to contemplate the role of the manse in 19th century English literature. Jane Austen had a clergyman for a father, as did the Bronte sisters, and that other popular but neglected writer, Joanna Baillie. Mary Brunton and Mrs Gaskell were both the wives of ministers. (John Buchan's son, as Mary McKerrow remarks in this book, always asserted that his father wrote so well because of the long boring hours spent listening every Sunday to his grandfather's long sermons.)

Self Control and *Discipline* sold immensely well at the time, though it may be a later generation of readers were put off by titles which suggested an unbearable degree ofVictorian respectability. But at the time they were written such titles gave permission to read. Encouraged by the reception of her work, begun so tentatively, to the extent that she refused to have her name on the title page of *Discipline*, lest it disgrace her husband, and her position and reputation amongst Edinburgh's gliteratti, Mary Brunton found the courage to call her next novel simply *Emmeline:* it was to tell the tale of a woman who leaves a loveless marriage to marry again, and of the savage social retribution which followed. It was to be the first of what was to be a series of 'domestic' novels. Alas, Mary Brunton was to die, tragically, in childbirth, before the book could be finished. But the novels remain as her memorial, of an intelligent, sensitive, witty, brave writer, whose work in the course of time may well enjoy another wave of critical attention. Just as *Mary Brunton, the forgotten Scottish novelist* – this loving appreciation of another writer's life, remains as Mary McKerrow's lasting memorial

Fay Weldon

Introduction

The opening pages of the biography of a best-selling 19th-century Scottish lady novelist, the wife of a minister of the Church of Scotland, may seem strangely detached from the expected story when it is seen that they feature the Huguenots, Henry of Navarre, Louis XIV of France, and battles long ago.

But French history is as closely associated with the life of Mary Brunton's mother's family, the Ligoniers, as is Orcadian history with Mary Brunton's father's family, the Balfours of Orkney.

Present-day visitors to Orkney who cross from Kirkwall to the island of Shapinsay and see over Balfour Castle may query the recurrence of the name Ligonier in connection with family pictures in the Portrait Gallery there. It is a name that has been handed down from generation to generation in one branch of the Balfour family after Frances, daughter of Colonel Francis (formerly Francoise-Auguste) Ligonier married Thomas Balfour, second son of William Balfour, 2nd Laird of Trenaby, in 1775, and in 1778 became the mother of Mary Brunton. The last Balfour to bear the Ligonier name was William Edward Ligonier Balfour, 7th Laird of Trenaby, who died in 1934.

The marriage between Frances, illegitimate daughter of Francoise-Auguste, and Thomas Balfour, was a union of two people whose fathers would never meet, each having been strongly loyal to opposing sides in the wars between the English and the Jacobites. While Francoise-Auguste was fighting the Jacobites on the field of Falkirk, William Balfour, a staunch Jacobite, was having his Orkney estates burnt to the ground by the English.

It took two generations, national disasters, military

involvements, and bitter family feuds before there emerged in Mary Balfour those qualities of Scottish and French culture, combined with the strong influence of her Presbyterian husband, which were to influence her success as a writer.

Her story has to be told against the background of this French and Scottish ancestry, traced through an Orkney childhood when her mother initiated her into the rudiments of French and Italian, and followed through the stormy maternal opposition to her dramatic elopement and subsequent marriage to a young minister of the Church of Scotland.

Reluctance to leave her first married home in the peaceful countryside of East Lothian for the bustle of life in Edinburgh was the needed catalyst for the flowering of her literary genius amongst the celebrated literati in the age of the Enlightenment.

Starting writing as a pastime, and being too self-effacing to tell her husband what she was doing until publication seemed inevitable, she refused to put her name on the title page of her first novel lest the adverse criticism that she was convinced would come, would have had a serious effect on her husband's established reputation as a minister of the prestigious Greyfriars Church.

The runaway success of the book in 1811 – 240 copies sold within five days of publication, and the remainder of the edition in demand in London – gave her sufficient confidence to start a second novel, which also enjoyed spectacular success when it appeared in 1815.

Both novels were re-issued in paperback in 1987 by Pandora Press. Extracts from Mary Brunton's journals of her English holidays in 1812 and 1815, are published here for the first time since in 1820 her husband selected and edited them after her death for inclusion in the issue of her third and unfinished novel, *Emmeline.*

Literate, beautifully descriptive, and often humorous, they form a unique, candid, and eager account of a young Scottish wife's impression of English customs, landscapes, cities, cathedrals and art treasures.

She recounts her infectious pleasure in recording in detail the making of such varied things as cannon-balls and button-eyes, the intricacies of silver-plating, porcelain manufacture, and the fortifications at Portsmouth, as well as the experience of sitting with her minister husband in the pit at Covent Garden to listen to an oratorio amongst a crowd of drunken sailors.

These human reactions, her zest for life, and her devotion to Christianity, made up the character of this gifted Scottish woman, destined not to live more than 40 years.

Family Tree of the Ligoniers

Louis Ligonier married Louise du Poncet - 28 March, 1677

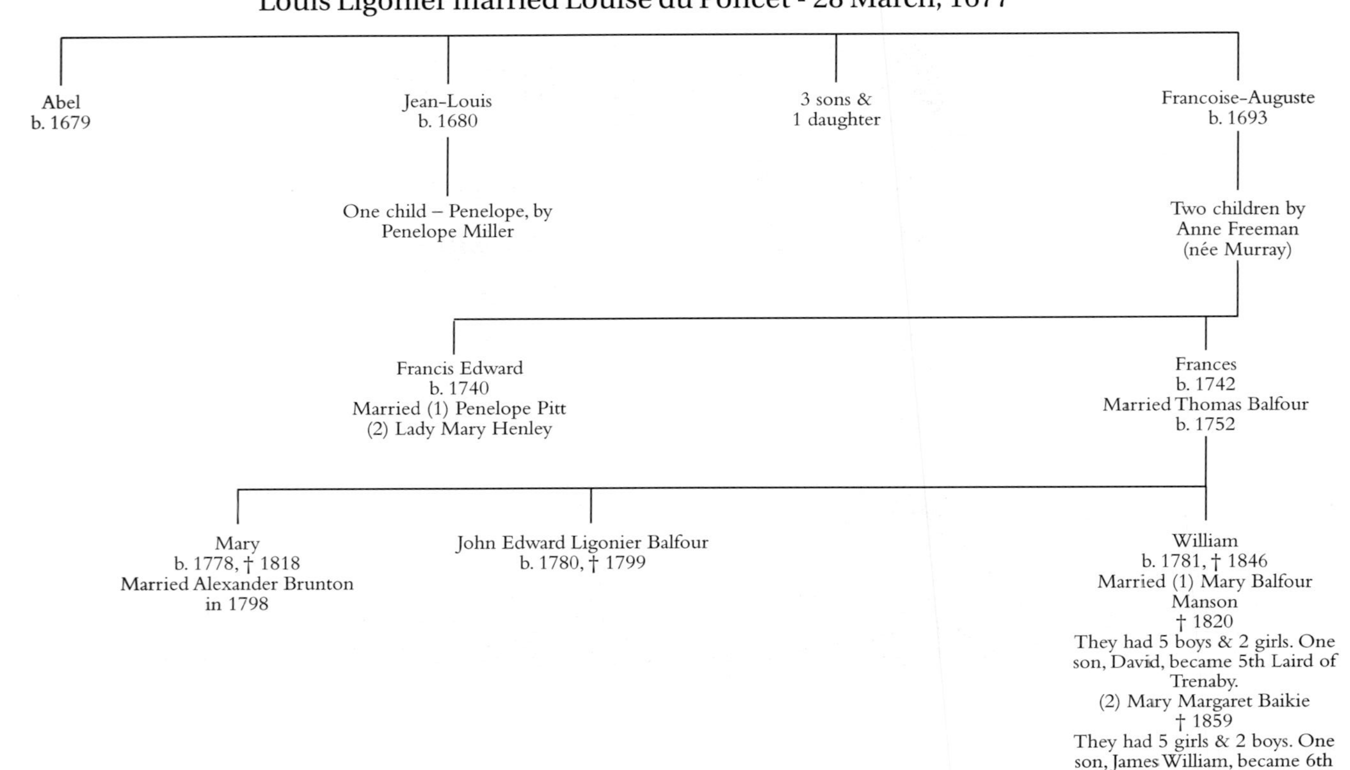

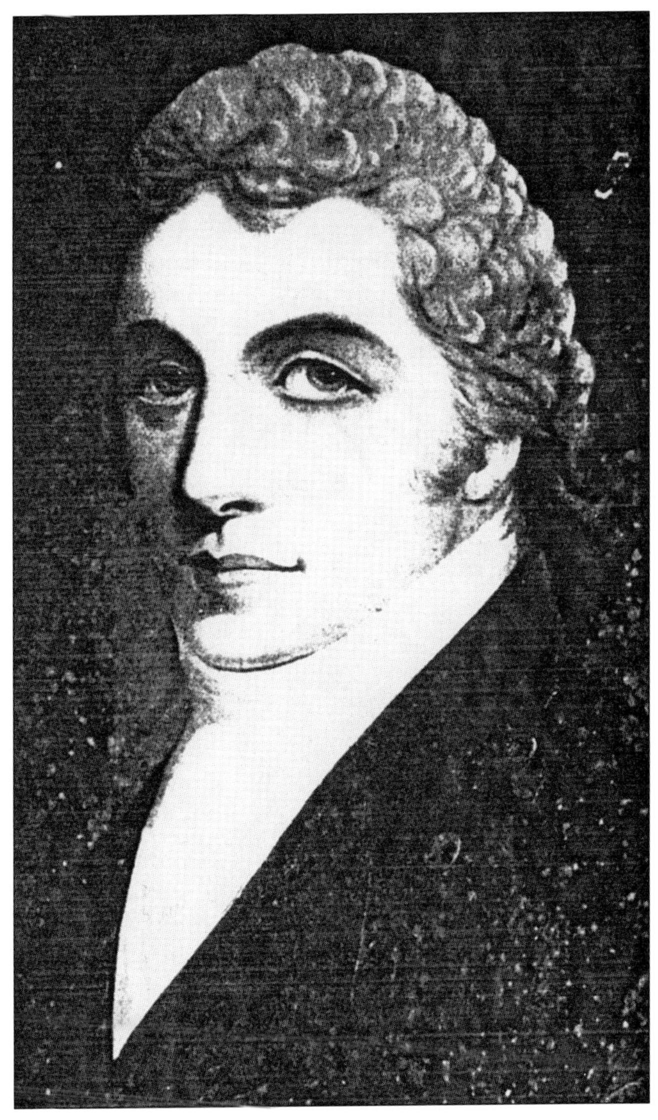

William Balfour of Balfour and Trenaby (1719-86)

Col. Thomas Balfour of Elwick (1752-99)

The Right Hon. John Lord Viscount Ligonier

Noltland Castle

Balfour Castle

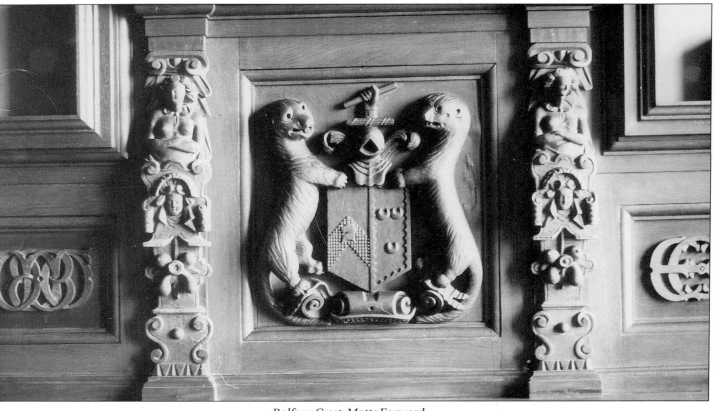

Balfour Crest: Motto Forward

Graveyard of the Balfours – Shapinsay

The Bu of Burray

The Liganiers

If it is unusual for a Frenchman to have his portrait in the Officers' Mess at Wellington Barracks, his bust by the celebrated sculptor Louis Roubillac in Windsor Castle, and his memorial in Westminster Abbey there must be a convincing explanation. How Field-Marshal Sir John Ligonier, Commander-in-Chief of the armed forces of King George II came to be so honoured for his achievements in England, and how he featured in the years before the life of his great-niece, Mary Brunton, is an integral part of this story.

The name Ligonier was a distinguished one in the British Army during the 18th century when Field-Marshal Ligonier's brother Francis was Colonel of the 13th Light Dragoons, and when Francis's son Edward was Colonel of the 9th Regiment of Foot. When Ensign Thomas Balfour of the 9th Foot married his Colonel's sister Frances Ligonier in 1777, he was marrying into one of the most famous military families in the country, and in due course became the father of Mary, the girl who was to be one of the best-selling Scottish novelists of the 19th century.

The Ligoniers first came to England as refugees, one of the many families of French Protestants, the Huguenots, who were driven from their native land by religious persecution. The Ligonier family came from Castres in Languedoc, east of Toulouse, a Huguenot stronghold with a cathedral and a thriving trade in woollens, soap and earthenware. One of the family, Antoine de Ligonier, had been mayor of the town before dying of the plague in 1570. He and his wife were among the many converts to Protestantism, and his descendants followed his beliefs.

The situation of the Huguenots seemed blessedly secure after the Protestant Henry of Navarre became king of France in 1589. To be allowed to take the throne, he had to become a Catholic, but was able to grant social and religious independence to all Huguenots by the Edict of Nantes, which became law on 13th April 1598. The protection of the Edict lasted almost a century, but continuing pressure by the Roman Catholic clergy culminated in Louis XIV's decision to revoke it on 18th October 1685.

Amongst the many Huguenots in Castres who felt the shock of the removal of the Edict were Louis de Ligonier and his wife Louise. Both came from the same well-to-do class of minor nobility, and were devout adherents to the Protestant faith. Happily married for eight years, they began to find their comfortable way of life drastically affected. Protestant churches were being demolished and they were no longer allowed to hold religious meetings in the privacy of their own homes, and all their ministers were ordered to leave the country within fourteen days. Their alarm increased when they learnt that they themselves could not leave the country without incurring the confiscation of all their property – a situation which could only be averted if they agreed to deny their faith and rear their children as Catholics.

Facing more than 400 proclamations, edicts and declarations, over 400,000 Huguenots sought sanctuary in England, Germany, the Netherlands and Switzerland. They left behind them the France of "le Roi de Soleil", the builder of Versailles, who paid a high price for revoking the Edict of Nantes. He lost many thousands of his best citizens; and the persecution of the French Protestants turned several other states against him, England amongst them. In 1688, the English drove out their Catholic King, James II, to bring in the Protestant William of Orange, who had led the United Provinces against Louis XIV's armies. In a few short years England had moved from being a wavering ally of France into her most determined enemy. She joined the League of Augsburg, which became the Grand Alliance of Vienna, under William's leadership, and the coalition of allies fought the French in a series of campaigns which over a period of twenty-five years marked a gradual decline of French power. In the early years following the revocation of the Edict of Nantes, about 70,000 of the French Protestant refugees came to England.

Louis de Ligonier could not escape, and remained in Castres where he died in 1693. For his first son, Abel, aged fourteen, there was the inheritance of the Monteuquet estate in Languedoc and the hereditary title of Seigneur de Monteuquet, as well as a town house from his mother's side of the family. For the second son, Jean-Louis, there was no inheritance. He stayed at home, but in early September 1698, when nearly eighteen, escaped to Holland to join one of his younger brothers at the home of their mother's brother in Utrecht.

After a few months there, he moved to Ireland in search of opportunity, knowing that there were Ligonier cousins in Dublin with military connections. After much thought, he decided to try joining the army, first as a soldier of fortune, fighting in battles under John Churchill, 1st Duke of Marlborough, in the series of brilliant victories that he achieved in the War of the Spanish Succession.

England, Holland and Austria were united in an effort to keep Louis from bringing Spain into his orbit, and a French advance towards Austria was driven back in confusion by Marlborough at Blenheim in 1703. At Ramillies in 1706, he totally routed the French, to transfer Flanders to the allies, and further victories at Oudenarde in 1708, and Malplaquet in 1709, marked the growing pressure on France that led to the Peace of Utrecht in 1712.

At Malplaquet, Jean-Louis Ligonier had a close escape from death when twenty-two shots were fired through his clothes.

By this time, he had made the decision to become a naturalised Englishman, made possible for him and many other refugees by an Act of Parliament. He paid the required small fee, and on 22nd February 1702, just over two months before the start of the war of the Spanish Succession, renounced his French nationality. Shortly afterwards he volunteered for service with the British forces in the Netherlands. At twenty-one years of age, he was one of the thousands of Huguenots who were becoming part of the backbone of the British Army. His new status gave him the confidence to try for an Army commission, aware that strength of character and courage were the usual requisites.

Able to prove that he possessed such requisites, he served with distinction under Marlborough, and became Lieutenant-Colonel of Horse in 1706, when he was 26. Four years later he was Major of Brigade in Spain, and in 1712, after being Assistant Adjutant-General to the Duke of Argyll, was promoted first Lieutenant-Colonel, and then Colonel of the 12th Foot.

But in spite of his English involvements, Colonel Ligonier still had a longing to see his family and particularly his youngest and favourite brother, Francoise-Auguste. Francoise needed little persuasion to join him, and soon found himself commissioned as an Ensign in the 12th Foot, serving side-by-side with Jean-Louis during the years when he was Lieutenant-Governor of Fort St Philip in Minorca from 1713-1716.

The prospect of returning to live in France became increasingly remote. Jean-Louis felt secure in his military position and it was already obvious that he and Francoise were both welcome in the country of their adoption. So they decided to anglicise their first names. Jean-Louis became John, and Francoise-Auguste became Francis. John had added to his prestige by entering the employment of the English royal family as Gentleman of the Privy Chamber to King George I. He was later to be aide-de-camp to King George II, a position which he held until his retirement.

Involvement amongst the higher ranks of society brings influential friends. One of these was the 2nd Duke of Argyll who had served in the War of the Spanish Succession and commanded the Government forces against the Jacobites in 1715. At John's request, he recommended Francis for a Cornetcy in the Royal Regiment of Horse Guards. The Duke's confidence was not unfounded when Francis was promoted to Major-General and then Lieutenant-Colonel.

The outbreak of the War of the Austrian Succession in 1740 brought both Ligoniers into the field against their former countrymen. The war, centred around the struggle for Silesia between Prussia and Austria, brought England and Holland together with Austria, once again against France. There can be few records, if any, of two French brothers commanding British forces in battles against their fellow-countrymen. John and Francis were at the forefront at Dettingen on 16 June 1743, when the British army, led by George II, defeated the French and drove them out of Germany. Both brothers were wounded. John, with the Dukes of Cumberland and Marlborough, was created Knight Banneret (an award for conspicuous gallantry which was presented on the field of battle). A month later he was made Knight of the Bath. Francis, Lieutenant-Colonel of the Light Dragoons, recovered from his wounds sufficiently to take on the Colonelcy of the 48th Foot in April 1745, and of the 13th Light Dragoons in September of the same year, while John was leading the 12th Foot at Fontenoy in Flanders. There, on 30th April 1745, the French forces under Marshal Saxe besieged Tournay and inflicted a heavy defeat upon the relieving English army led by the Duke of Cumberland, later to be the notorious 'butcher of Culloden'.

Away from the battlefields, the two French brothers, with the traditional gallantry of their nation, as well as their officers' uniforms and their now almost legendary heroism, were an inescapable target for the ladies. Each formed romantic attachments, although neither married. John, at the age of 47, fathered a daughter, Penelope, by Penelope Miller, a lady from Southwark, and reared the child as if she was legitimate. In due course this daughter Penelope married Arthur Graham of County Armagh, who became Lieutenant-Colonel of the 1st Regiment of Foot Guards. They had six children, the eldest son being named Ligonier Arthur Graham, to whom John was to leave £10,000 in his will.

Francis had two children by a widow called Anne Freeman. Their son, Francis Edward, was born in 1740, and their daughter, Frances, in 1742. Finding himself now in the position of a family man, he took stock of his financial situation. Two years after his daughter's birth, when in Brussels, he made a will "to settle how my worldly goods shall be disposed in case I should be such a fool as to die". He reckoned that his whole estate was worth £1,300 and his "equipage" (if not lost) £300.

Two years later he was "'fool enough to die" after commanding the 48th Foot and the 13th Light Dragoons at the Battle of Falkirk in the bitter Scottish winter of 1746. At Falkirk 9,000 Hanoverians under General Hawley met 8,000 Jacobites with Prince Charles Edward at their head. Hawley, regarded as a pig-headed disciplinarian with little time for undisciplined rabbles, was, somewhat surprisingly, taking breakfast with the Jacobite Countess of Kilmarnock, whose husband, the 4th Earl, had been Privy Councillor to Prince Charles Edward. After repeated requests as to the General's whereabouts, he eventually rode up in a fury, grey hair streaming in the wind, in time to see the Jacobites advancing towards a hill south-west of Falkirk.

Hawley ordered his dragoons, under Francis Ligonier, to seize the height, with the Foot to follow. But the storm that beat in the faces of the soldiers as they charged up the hill was too severe for them to be able to protect their weapons from the heavy rain. With fixed bayonets they met the Highlanders who were first to the top. Hawley, sword in hand, ordered the dragoons to advance, only to see them receiving a volley at 10 or 12 paces, wheeling round and galloping out of sight. The infantry was so disordered that the Highlanders could pursue them down the hill, flourishing their broadswords. But for the rally of a few scattered battalions and two unbroken regiments, the English army would have been annihilated. The Jacobites, triumphant after their humiliating retreat from Derby, claimed the day.

Many of the survivors, including Francis Ligonier, suffered from exposure after the battle. A week later, on 25 January 1746, he died of pleurisy and was buried on 28 January in Edinburgh. He was 53, leaving behind a son of five and a daughter of three. The Holyrood Burial Register records: 'Collonel Lergonier [*sic*] at the middle of the large window in the east end of the church'. No tombstone can be found.

John, now 65, was so deeply involved as Commander-in-Chief of the five-year campaign in Flanders with a period of such high activity and intense concentration that he was spared, if only temporarily, from a terrible personal grief. Only when, at Lauffeld, he was for the first time in his life taken prisoner following the defeat of the British Army under the Duke of Cumberland, did he have time to think about his loss.

He had been cordially received by the French king, Louis XV, when taken into captivity. The king came face to face with this courageous Frenchman, driven from his homeland by the religious persecution perpetrated by Louis XIV, and now a hero in his adopted country. There is a mention of this battle in Smollett's *History of England* telling how at one point defeat for the

Hanoverians looked imminent and the Duke of Cumberland was in danger of being taken prisoner, when John Ligonier risked himself and some of his troops for the safety of the rest of the army. At the head of three British regiments of dragoons and some squadrons of Imperial Horse, he charged the whole line of the French cavalry with such ferocity that he overthrew all challengers and made it possible for the Duke of Cumberland to retreat. Only when his horse was killed under him was he taken prisoner by a French carabineer.

After his release, following the peace of Aix-la-Chapelle in 1748, he was overcome with remorse and guilt at having persuaded Francis to come to England and join the army and meet his death. His only expiation seemed to lie in the care of Francis's little son and daughter who were only five and three when their father died. His London house in North Audley Street would be their home, and there they would be brought up in the company of his own daughter, the teenage Penelope, in a way fitting for the children of the Colonel of a British regiment. He was determined to manage this, although he was past what would be the retirement age of today. His public involvements had increased rather than decreased; he became Lieutenant-General of the Ordnance two years after Francis died, and its Master-General from 1759-63; and thereafter Whig Member of Parliament for Bath, Privy Councillor, Fellow of the Royal Society, Governor of the French Hospital in London, and Governor of Guernsey and of Plymouth. And he continued to fulfil his duties as Colonel of the Royal Horse Guards and the 1st Foot Guards.

At the age of 77 he was created Viscount of Enniskillen, Co. Fermanagh, Ireland, taking his title from the country where he first decided on a military career. On 20 May 1762, when he was 81, he became Viscount Ligonier of Clonmell, and less than a year later was created a Peer of Great Britain as Lord Ligonier, Baron of Ripley in the county of Surrey. When he finally resigned his office of Field-Marshal and Commander-in-Chief in Great Britain, he was created Earl Ligonier.

He had liked the look of Cobham Place in Surrey in the years before he became a Field-Marshal, and decided to buy it four years after Francis died because it seemed a good place for the young people to go to when they wanted a change from London. He kept a pack of hounds at this attractive residence which had previously been Cobham Park, belonging to a family called Downe for several generations. Here he retired after his last public appearance in his eightieth year, when he had marched at the head of the military parade at the coronation of George III and received a tremendous ovation. Compared with other Frenchmen of his time he was described as "polished from foppery by age and by living in a more thinking country". Universally beloved and respected, modest and unassuming, he asked on his death that he be buried near to Cobham Place in an unmarked grave. But after he died on 27th April 1770 in his 90th year, the public, unwilling to see their French hero pass into oblivion, erected a memorial to him in Westminster Abbey, listing his honours:

Baron Ripley in Surrey
Viscount of Inniskillin and Viscount of Clonmell
Field Marshal and Commander-in-Chief His Majesty's Forces
Master General of the Ordnance
Colonel lst Regiment of Foot Guards
Privy Councillor
Knight of the Bath.

The Ligonier name survives in a street in London. After the arrival of the Huguenots in England in the 17th century, many chose to live in the Soho and Spitalfields areas – the stronghold of non-conformity – where the lease of a chapel was granted to a French congregation. After the silk-weaving industry – always an attraction to the French – moved from Spitalfields to Bethnal Green, a street there was named Ligonier Street which, significantly, happily, and surely not just by chance, runs into a street named Navarre.

Not in London alone do people comment on this unusual name. Visitors to Balfour Castle on the Orkney island of Shapinsay see pictures of the first Earl Ligonier in the Portrait Gallery. Those who go to the Exhibition Centre at Fort George in the county of Inverness will see a quotation from a statement made by Lord Ligonier when Commander-in-Chief. The fort was built after

Culloden as the Highland Garrison Fortress for the Hanoverian army of George II, with work beginning in 1748 and finishing in 1769 at a cost of more than £200,000. As the Jacobites had taken Fort William and Fort Augustus in the '45 rebellion, the idea behind Fort George was to provide a strong base in the Highlands which could be provisioned and reinforced by sea in the event of fresh trouble. Lord Ligonier, knowing the French, always felt that they might try to stir up more action in the Highlands and, rather hoping that they would make an attempt on the seeming impregnability of Fort George, wrote the words which are exhibited there today:

> *I shall be extremely glad that they would do it because I look upon the Fort as impregnable against any force that could be sent against it.*

Dr Johnson and James Boswell dined there in 1773 as the guests of the 37th Regiment on the narrow spit of land where the waters of the Inner and Outer Loch Moray meet, and were struck with admiration 'at finding upon this barren sandy point such buildings, such a dinner, such company: it was like enchantment'.

Edward Ligonier, John's nephew and Francis's son, was in his 30th year when he succeeded to the title of Viscount Ligonier on the death of his uncle in 1770. John had allowed him £75 a quarter and bought him a commission in the 1st Foot Guards after he had served during five campaigns in the Seven Years' War under Prince Ferdinand of Brunswick. He had carried the despatch which announced the famous victory of Minden on 1 August 1759, when he was 19, and had become aide-de-camp to King George III in 1763, Secretary to the Embassy in Madrid from 1763-65, and Groom of the Bedchamber to the Duke of Gloucester.

By the age of 26 he was an attractive marriage proposition, and when Penelope Pitt, daughter of the 1st Baron Rivers and his wife Penelope, fell in love with him (or with the idea of becoming a Viscountess) they were married at the British Embassy in Paris on 16 December 1766. She was nine years younger than he. All appeared to go well with the marriage until she began to have a torrid affair with the romantic Count Vittorio Amadeo Alfieri, more her own age. Edward, predictably furious with Penelope for openly flaunting her affair and casting a shadow of scandal on the Ligonier name, tried to stave off the shame of the inevitable divorce until after his uncle's death. He was not prepared for the embarrassment which his uncle's will produced when he found that he and Penelope were to receive £20,000 as a marriage settlement which would go to John's daughter Penelope were they to die without issue. But neither this generous bequest, nor Edward's title, could lure Penelope back. Hurt and angry, Edward did what he considered the honourable thing and challenged Alfieri to a duel in London's Green Park in the May of 1771, borrowing a sword from a cutler in Bond Street for the purpose. Neither was mortally wounded and the duel only served to increase Alfieri's status in Penelope's eyes. Her divorce from Edward was finalised by an Act of Parliament on 7 November 1771.

Apart from making his name in Italy for bringing patriotism, sincerity and tragedy into the national drama scene, Alfieri, during his association with Penelope, started writing the first of his nineteen tragedies portraying the struggle against moral and political tyranny, one of which he dedicated to George Washington, 'the liberator of America', not to mention five sonnets called *L'AmericaLibera,* celebrating America's newly-acquired independence. Count Alfieri's literary and political outbursts had been enough to entice Penelope away from the shackles of a conventional marriage, but seem to have failed to provide lasting satisfaction. A few years after their divorce, Edward read that she was having an affair with a postilion which was highlighted in the 1777 publication of *The Electric Eel,* perhaps the 18th century equivalent of today's *Private Eye.* The two-line piece of topical chat made no secret of it:

But see the luscious Ligonier
Prefers her post-boy to her peer.

Penelope was sufficiently 'luscious' to have her portrait painted by Gainsborough. Years after, when Edward had died and his second wife had re-married and become Viscountess Wentworth, she told her sister-in-law, Frances Balfour (née Ligonier) that she had been reading *The Life of Count Alfieri* who had recently died.

In it he referred to Frances as the 'belle soeur' to Penelope at whose house they had met. Mary Wentworth had little time for the Count:

> *He is Count All-Fiery, as the vulgars used to call him, and I wonder she escaped with her life . . . He was supposed to be privately married to the Countess of Albany . . . I never saw the hero. Was he handsome and clever?*

Frances lost no time in telling Lady Wentworth that he was no Adonis. Army involvements for Edward were, as his uncle John had found before him, a release from personal problems, and, following the Ligonier style, he advanced from Lieutenant-Colonel to Colonel of the 9th Regiment of Foot. Two years after his divorce from Penelope he married Lady Mary Henley, third daughter of the lst Earl of Northington and his wife Jane. This marriage was a success, but Edward's hopes of having children were disappointed again, and the £20,000 marriage settlement from John's will may have reverted to Penelope Graham and her family after all.

In the Army Lists for 1777, on the same page as Edward's promotion to Lieutenant-General, there appears, for the first time, the name of the newest Ensign in the 9th Regiment of Foot – Thomas Balfour – as from 2nd March 1776, the year in which Edward was created Earl Ligonier of Clonmell. Twenty months after this, Thomas's first child, Mary, was born.

The friendship between Thomas Balfour and his Colonel's sister, Frances Ligonier, began either when he was a civilian, (and he joined Edward's regiment because of it), or after his enlistment, and was a whirlwind romance. Frances had been allowed £100 a year by her Uncle John and she was trained in French, Italian and music, accomplishments which she was to pass on to her daughter Mary. When the scandal of Penelope's affair with Alfieri broke she was nearly 30, and it only served to strengthen her closeness to her brother which had grown with the passing of the years. Under Uncle John's will she had received £2,000. She had a house in London, plenty of friends who admired her wit and original conversation and her brilliant gift for music and languages which ensured a safe entrée into society gatherings. But in spite of these talents, she was in danger of qualifying for the 'confirmed spinster' label. A childhood spent without a conventionally stable background since the age of three, and the death of her heroic father at Falkirk, had developed a trace of hardness and a suspicion of romantic attachments. Her knowledge of what happened to children when left alone through death had brought on an early bitterness when she dwelt on the image of her gallant father whom she had hardly known. His example, and that of her celebrated uncle, seems to have fired her with a great sense of duty and a strong belief in the virtue of army officers. There was little doubt in the minds of her friends that, were Frances ever to marry, she would not be looking far beyond a figure that was wearing an army officer's uniform. She would consider it a duty to the memory of her father and her uncle to marry into the army.

This strong sense of duty guided many of her future actions. Her show of brightness at army social gatherings – often the requisite for acceptability and popularity – may have cloaked feelings of desolation, unaccountable worry and self-doubt, problems which in later life were to be the cause of many family difficulties.

As the sister of the Colonel, she rarely failed to appear at social military gatherings. She mingled with the officers and their wives and often, being rather a lonely person herself, singled out the newest officers to talk to, trying to make them relaxed and more confident if necessary. When talking to the young Ensign Thomas Balfour, she discovered not only that his home was in the far-off Orkney Islands, which was interesting in itself, but also that she was being drawn into discussion on her favourite subjects of music, poetry and the novels of the day. When it emerged that this young man owed his descent to a long line of Balfours with a military history even longer than that of the Ligoniers, her interest quickened. Even though her father had died fighting in Scotland, she had little knowledge of Scottish history and had to admit that she knew nothing of the Balfours who bled with Wallace, or of those who had fought at Neville's Cross in 1345, at Roxburgh in 1460, or at Branxton Moor with James IV in 1513. The news that the army involvement of the Balfours stretched further back into history than that of the Ligoniers seemed to put the Colonel's sister on to a more equal footing with this young man from Orkney.

Their meetings became more frequent. On the surface it would appear that her attraction for him arose out of shared interests, but, looking below the surface, we see a woman of 34, with marriage prospects fast disappearing, meeting a man, ten years her junior, with all the appeal that a Scotsman has for an Englishwoman, and all the interests to match her own. That he was exceptionally well-educated, had a military career ahead, and was a member of an historic family in the islands to the north, brought a romantic and appealing flavour to the association.

Thomas Balfour, at the age of 24, with an Ensign's pay of three shillings and eightpence with three extra shillings for subsistence, could not fail to be flattered by his Colonel's sister's apparent interest in him. Whereas he welcomed the opportunity for academic discussion after his time at Aberdeen University and Edinburgh University where he had studied for a medical degree before joining the army, there was much to be considered before any firm and permanent involvement could happen. He had changed from thoughts of a medical career to that of an army officer when the American War of Independence brought young men flocking to the colours. When he enlisted with the 9th Regiment of Foot, America, he had money problems which marriage with the Colonel's sister might solve. But even if marriage with a lady from the upper echelons of London society were to endow him with personal kudos, he still had to weigh up the reactions in Orkney when his near and dear relations saw him bring home, as his bride, a lady ten years too old. But the Balfours had rarely rejected a challenge, and Thomas, praying that Frances would have a good reception in Orkney, asked her to marry him.

She accepted with little delay, finding a sense of security in seeing behind her future husband the same tradition of military service that she had been brought up to revere. In accepting Thomas's proposal she may have felt that she was keeping faith with the father she had barely known, and with the uncle who had cared for her, and, by becoming the wife of an officer in her brother's regiment and the daughter-in-law of the laird of Trenaby in the Orkney Islands, she was justifying her existence.

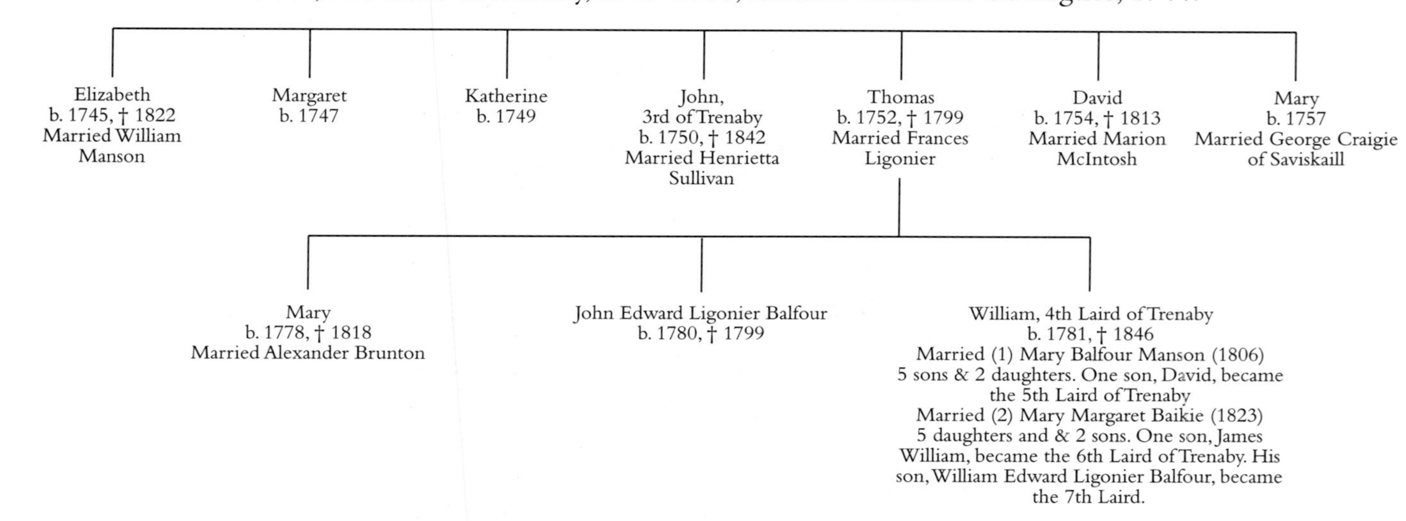
Family Tree of the Balfours
William Balfour, 2nd Laird of Trenaby, 1719-1786, married Elizabeth Covingtrie, 1744.
Elizabeth b. 1745, † 1822 Married William Manson
Margaret b. 1747
Katherine b. 1749
John, 3rd of Trenaby b. 1750, † 1842 Married Henrietta Sullivan
Thomas b. 1752, † 1799 Married Frances Ligonier
David b. 1754, † 1813 Married Marion McIntosh
Mary b. 1757 Married George Craigie of Saviskaill
Mary b. 1778, † 1818 Married Alexander Brunton
John Edward Ligonier Balfour b. 1780, † 1799
William, 4th Laird of Trenaby b. 1781, † 1846 Married (1) Mary Balfour Manson (1806) 5 sons & 2 daughters. One son, David, became the 5th Laird of Trenaby Married (2) Mary Margaret Baikie (1823) 5 daughters and & 2 sons. One son, James William, became the 6th Laird of Trenaby. His son, William Edward Ligonier Balfour, became the 7th Laird.

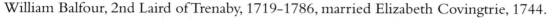

The Balfours of Orkney

While Francis Ligonier was fighting his final battle for the Hanoverians against the Jacobites at Falkirk in 1746, William Balfour was fiercely supporting the Jacobites in Orkney. These two, dramatically opposed in their loyalties, were the grandfathers of the girl who was born Mary Balfour and became Mary Brunton.

Death removed Francis from any personal loss or gain as a result of the hostilities. William's Trenaby estate, to which he had succeeded as the second laird on the death of his father, John Balfour, in 1742, was burnt to the ground because of his allegiance to Prince Charles Edward Stuart. Bankruptcy followed, and it was only through the practical support of his wife, Elizabeth Covingtrie, and his own determination, that he was able to re-establish himself as a respected and influential laird.

The Covingtries were an Orkney family. William Covingtrie settled in the islands in 1613. David Covingtrie of Eynhallow, Elizabeth's grandfather, was Chamberlain to Bishop Murdo MacKenzie, the last of the bishops during the episcopacy in Orkney from 1660-1689, and her father, Thomas, was licensed as a minister by the Presbytery of Kirkwall in 1711. His first charge was at Newark, Sanday, where he grew in stature in Orkney society by marrying Elspeth Loutitt, daughter of the Provost of Kirkwall.

Elizabeth brought wealth to her marriage with William. Her wise use of it then, and in the years that followed, was a strong factor in consolidating the fortunes of this branch of the Balfour family which was to flourish for over 200 years. On the Findhaven estate in the county of Angus there is a covin-tree, said to have been grown from a chestnut dropped by a Roman soldier. It is an unusual name, with indications of solidarity and longevity, characteristics with which Elizabeth Covingtrie was well endowed.

Her father was as dedicated a Jacobite as William. Indignant at the degradation that his son-in-law had suffered, he joined him and three others, Archibald Stewart of Brugh, John Traill of Westness and John Traill of Elsness (all sufferers during the Jacobite Rebellion), in hiding in a cave at Noup Head on the north side of Westray which became known as 'The Gentlemen's Ha'. There they wintered in freezing conditions, afraid to light a fire for fear of being discovered by smoke arising above the Westray cliffs. William Sinclair, tenant of the Bu in Rapness, got a young girl to lower supplies to them in a basket from the cliff above the cave at great risk to herself. After their escape, William, in gratitude, sent a set of silver spoons to the young girl, and was deeply moved when they were returned to him at her request when she was dying.

Any good repute that the Balfours may have had before the Jacobite Rebellion had been largely eclipsed by the scandalous behaviour of Gilbert Balfour, brother-in-law of Adam Bothwell, Archbishop of Orkney from 1559. He craftily used this relationship to get himself selected to visit Rome to obtain the papal bull appointing Adam to the Archbishopric, and on his return, demanded to be rewarded for his efforts with the huge feu of church lands in Westray, Papa Westray, and later, a much-disputed, but equally extensive grant of land at Birsay and Marwick.

Orcadians, deeply concerned, saw religious feudalism threatening to sweep the islands, not comparable with the religious persecution that the Ligoniers had to suffer in France a century later, but serious enough. They saw this greedy acquisition of church land by those outwith the church as a serious threat to their way of life. There were no martyrs, no mass emigration, but the unrest grew. Few could forget that Gilbert Balfour, involved in the murder of Cardinal David Beaton in 1546, had earned a spell on the French galleys with John Knox as a fellow-prisoner. Sensing the strength of public feeling against him, and aware that his life was forfeit, he built Noltland Castle as his bolt-hole, a stronghold against public reaction for a man with a bad conscience and fear in his heart. Constructed between 1560 and 1573, 71 yawning gun-loops still pierce the outer walls in all directions, more than in any other Scottish castle. Everything shows a desperate need for security in the mind of a man with many enemies. The main staircase, one of the finest in Scotland, has a newel with a carved capital including the double-headed eagle of the Holy Roman Empire, and at the top, a guard-chamber with gun-loops commanding the stairhead and the passage into the main hall.

But Gilbert had little opportunity to enjoy Noltland. After getting himself elected Sheriff of Orkney and Captain of Kirkwall Castle in 1567, and Master of Queen Mary's Household after she returned from France, he became involved in the conspiracy to murder Henry Stuart, Lord Darnley, second husband of the Queen. In the Parliament of 1571, he was found guilty of treason and fled to Sweden. Noltland Castle was no longer a safe refuge. Priding himself that he could get away with a conspiracy to cause the death of the Swedish king, he was discovered, captured, and executed.

Noltland Castle lay neglected after his hurried departure, but 100 years later it was the scene of a happy occasion – the marriage of George Balfour of Pharay to his first wife, Margaret Baikie, daughter of James Baikie of Tankerness. The celebrations, as at all good Scottish weddings, went on and on, even after strong gales arose and prevented the guests from leaving for literally weeks. The steward was eventually forced to announce that every beast had been killed except the bull. George Balfour, never one to spoil a party, ordered that to be slain also. Whatever gods were responsible for whipping up the storm must have been placated by such a sacrifice, for the wind abated and the guests were able to depart. George was a popular and good-looking man, six foot two in his socks. After Margaret Baikie died he married Mary MacKenzie, only daughter of Bishop Murdo MacKenzie. Their son, John, was the first laird of Trenaby. His grandson William was the second laird, and George and Mary were the great-great-grandparents of Mary Balfour whose other great-great grandfather, David Covingtrie, had been Bishop MacKenzie's Chamberlain.

During the 18th century, William Balfour, recovered from his brush with the anti-Jacobites, became a public benefactor. When the hurricane of 1756 blasted the Orkney corn crop and caused a shortage of meal in Westray, he supplied the area with about 20 tons of potatoes, telling Elizabeth to "cry them at the Kirk on

Sunday to be sold on Monday". Mary Balfour was seven years old when he died, but those who believe in heredity might think that in later life she had inherited from her grandfather his fascination with the manipulation of words. A rare example of William's succinct turn of phrase comes in an extract from his letter to Elizabeth from London:

> *You will have heard of the death of His Royal Highness the Duke of York; it is said here, he was stabd (sic) through the body and his Paramoor with him, in the embraces of the Lady, whose Husband took this method of repairing his honour upon both offenders and both are dead as they deserve.*

William and Elizabeth's first child was a daughter, Elizabeth, born 1745. The hoped-for son was stillborn in 1746. Two more daughters followed, Margaret, in 1747, and the short-lived Katherine in 1747, before a healthy son arrived in 1750. They named him John after William's father. This boy was to have a strongly beneficial influence on the fortunes of the Balfour family. Two more sons followed him in quick succession, Thomas (1752) who joined the British Army and became the father of Mary Balfour, and David (1753) who became a Writer to the Signet in Edinburgh.

After giving birth to seven children in eight years, Elizabeth gave herself a short break before producing another daughter, Mary, in 1757. This girl became the favourite aunt of Mary Balfour, and, prior to her marriage to George Craigie of Saviskaill, was presented at Court. The letter which she wrote to her sister Elizabeth describing her experiences that day is in the Archives Department of the Orkney Library in Kirkwall. Undated, and sparsely punctuated, it vividly brings to life, after 200 years, the ordeal of a young Orkney girl when plunged into London society:

> *It is all over with me my dear Betty I have been at Court and done nothing and what have I recourse to now I know not heaven direct me and why not call heaven to my aid it is a serious matter and the world can do no more for me. There was I, dressed out in my best flowered silk sack which I have not had above seven*

years with the plaits of the gown and petticoat . . . to make it receive a hoop for no lady of rank (observe) goes without one. My hair dress'd out to such a size that I declare my head appear'd to me almost as big as my whole body at least . . . a good large cap on the top of all yet it was moderate compared with many. I sat there with Lady Ligonier's jewels and some other things of hers which were better than I had of my own and put on by her own hands which was more than she would have done for herself but she is one of the best-natured women alive and full of that pride which is so common in people of rank and which they take every opportunity of showing to their inferiors. I hope you don't think me such a fool as really to appear even where I was a stranger in all the jewels that Lady Ligonier might appear in, but her diamond ear-rings and necklace I had much against my inclination for fear of any accident happening to them, but she would not be refused with all these advantages. Lord Ligonier told me I was a bonny lass tonight and I am sure His Lordship can't flatter with all these advantages . . . While I am confined to a sheet of paper it is vain to attempt giving a description. A very good way to get off, say you, not being very good at giving descriptions I can only tell you that it was a most brilliant assembly. A great many very fine women elegantly dress'd. The men upon the whole very plain tho' I heard of one suit being embroider'd with french paste and other stones to resemble diamonds. The King and Queen were very plain in their dress. Her Majesty is a very fine figure of a woman in my opinion and a sweet-looking woman but not a good feature on her face. The king is a jolly-looking man. He seems good-natured and affable . . . We saw none of the young royal family.

Ever yours,
M. BALFOUR.

Frances Balfour, sister of Lord Ligonier, who had married Thomas Balfour when Mary was nineteen, initiated this invitation to Court for her young sister-in-law, hoping that it would give her a taste for the kind of life in London which she herself had enjoyed as a girl, but without success.

William Balfour had attended Kirkwall Grammar School,

founded in 1544 by Bishop Robert Reid, one of the most outstanding churchmen of his century who died in 1558 and left a legacy for a college to be erected in Edinburgh. Twenty years after his death the money was used to establish the University of Edinburgh, which, in 1813, was to appoint Alexander Brunton, husband of William's granddaughter, Mary, as Professor of Hebrew and Oriental Languages.

William's three sons attended Kirkwall Grammar School, proceeding to Aberdeen University, whence they all emerged as "Alumni and Graduates in Arts" in the University's records for 1766 and 1771. William accepted the post of factor in Shetland when offered by the influential Sir Laurence Dundas, a Director of the East India Company, which encouraged him to put forward his eldest son John's name for the position of Writer in the East India Company. So, at the age of twenty-one, John Balfour set foot on the coast of Coromandel and took his first steps towards acquiring the fortune which was to put the Balfours in the forefront of Orkney life for many years to come. On 20 April 1771, he wrote to his sister Betty:

> *I suppose you have heard that it is resolved that I shall go to the East Indies and that I am to return in a short time a Nabob with a fortune of at least £5,000 if my stars be kind, with much more.*

William died in 1786 and John became the 3rd laird of Trenaby. At the age of thirty-six he was an Auditor for the East India Company. Astute and business-like, no sufferer of fools, and never slow to seize his opportunities, endowed with the increasing confidence which wealth often brings, he stood for Parliament, and was elected Member for Orkney in 1790, remaining its representative for the next six years. Standing again in 1820, when nearly 70, he was elected for another six years. His constituency had a population of 53,124. Much of his money he ploughed back into Orkney. By buying the estate of William Honyman (the judge, Lord Armadale) for £34,000 and another local property, he became only second in rank to Lord Zetland as an Orkney landowner. Lord Zetland allowed him to buy out his feu duties for £5,551, so making the Balfour estates free to grow less grain and rear more cattle.

This made it possible to exploit the improving conditions of communication with the south and gradually shift production to a commodity more efficiently produced in the Orkney climate.

For Members of Parliament, a London residence was desirable. John chose prestigious premises at 18 Curzon Street, Mayfair, and a country property at Old Charlton, overlooking the Thames. His main object as a Parliamentarian was to see that his Orkney constituents had a fair deal. In 1837, when he was 88, he sent £100 to help those of his tenants who were in desperate need of corn and potatoes after severe weather had made it impossible for their crops to ripen. Constant July rain had interrupted the kelp-making and stopped its manufacture until the herring fishing, which was developing well, began again. Kelp, the source of wealth which came from the burning of seaweed from which alkali was extracted for use in the manufacture of soap and glass, and for the bleaching of linen, was vitally important in Orkney. Formerly looked upon as just a valuable fertiliser, its importance was heightened when it was realised that it could fetch £6 a ton and bring in a revenue of £10,000. During the French wars, the revenue rose to £20,000 and agriculture began to be neglected as a result. Kelp-burning in Orkney died out after the First World War.

John Balfour's marriage to Henrietta, sister of Sir Richard Sulliven, was childless – a source of great disappointment to this immensely wealthy man. As his riches grew, so did speculation within the Balfour family as to his chosen heir. Not only financially, but also morally, John was the man who revived the Balfour pride after the disasters of the Jacobite rebellion. His strength lay in his character – strong, uncompromising, rational, sometimes ironical, but always full of common sense. Only an exceptional man with the right qualities could be chosen to run his Orkney estates in a way that he approved.

The early death of his younger brother Thomas at the age of 46 excluded him from the succession. His career after Aberdeen University had moved from academic studies to military involvement, and finally to a successful farming life in Orkney. At Edinburgh University, he had been one of the sixteen graduates in the medical class of 1774 when he took as the subject for his thesis "De Cortice Peruviano" – the study of the Peruvian variety of the cinchona, a tree of the South American rubiaceous genus, cinchona, especially the cinchona calisaya which has a medicinal bark which when dried, yields quinine and other medicinal alkaloids. But it was probably the American War of Independence that led Thomas, like many other young men, to join the army in England. Only when circumstances there became difficult did the pull of Orkney become irresistible. John was relieved to see his brother back, welcoming him as a man of vision and enterprise when he saw him build a fine house for his family on Shapinsay and improve the standard of living for his tenants.

With the arrival of Thomas's two sons he saw a sign of hope for an heir for himself. Were they to be brought up as Orkney-lovers and estate managers, one of them would surely develop the qualities that he was looking for.

But Thomas, his wife Frances, and their elder son, John Edward Ligonier Balfour, were all dead by the time that John Balfour, now approaching seventy years of age, had the urgent need to decide on the final allocation of his fortune. Mary Balfour, the eldest child of Thomas and Frances, even if eligible, was soon to die also. William, their younger son, now aged 36, was the one who now came under the microscope. John desperately wanted a near Balfour relation whom he could trust to follow in his footsteps, and, William, as his nephew, his nearest relative, emerged as the most likely candidate.

After schooling in Harrow, William had succeeded in his request to become "anything but a lawyer", and joined the Navy. Wounded in two of the thirteen engagements in which he took part during the French Revolutionary and Napoleonic Wars, and emerging with a record of hard work and determination, he gained the rank of Lieutenant-Commander at the age of 24. Only when he became aware that political changes were altering the system of promotion in the Navy and that his further advancement was suffering as a consequence did he leave the service in disgust in 1808 with the rank of Captain, and never went to sea again. There was another more personal reason for this also. All William wanted to do on leaving the Navy was to settle down in Orkney with the wife he had married two years previously, Mary Balfour Manson, daughter of William Manson, Comptroller of Customs in Kirkwall, and

Elizabeth Manson, his father's eldest sister. They lived in the family home, Cliffdale, and had five sons in ten years. The first, named John after his rich great-uncle, was born on 1 August 1807, a first grandchild for William's mother Frances. But, worn out with child-bearing, Mary died when her youngest son, George Craigie Balfour, was two years old.

William adapted himself well to the life of a minor Orkney laird, was popular with his tenants, and reasonably well off as a retired Navy Officer on half-pay, receiving rents from the Shapinsay tenants and a share of the kelp production. The wealthy uncle John viewed such thrifty habits with approval, and cautiously began to wonder if he had at last found his Balfour heir. To test him, he gave him the job of factor on his extensive Orkney estates, discovering in so doing that his nephew was scrupulously fair in all his dealings and unfailingly honest. A man after his own heart, and one whom he had despaired of finding.

But caution still ruled his decisions. His brother Thomas had died in the prime of life. Thomas's elder son had died in battle before he was 20, and William's firstborn son had died of convulsions at a year old after vaccination in 1808 in Kirkwall, a place not then renowned for its hygiene. Such events made Uncle John see the need to plan beyond William for his heir lest William met with an early death also. He therefore studied the qualities of William's son, Thomas, educated in Liverpool and at Cambridge University where he suffered concussion in a severe riding accident which had interrupted his studies. But on recovery he studied law, and became an Advocate in 1832, practising in Edinburgh until fired with the ambition of entering Parliament at the age of twenty-five. The thought of seeing another Balfour at Westminster greatly pleased Uncle John and he began to view this young man as his possible heir, should William prematurely die. He financed Thomas's political campaign, and experienced a great sense of satisfaction when he was elected Member of Parliament for Orkney and Shetland in 1835. He worked hard, and was popular in his constituency during the famine in the bad winter of 1837, when he actively helped those islanders who were without food.

But after two years, disenchantment set in. Requests from the public made him impatient; he was always short of money, and longed to be independent of his obligation to his uncle, and free to marry Eleanor Edmeston to whom he had been engaged for several years. By 1837 he was talking of quitting politics and helping his father on Uncle John's estates in the summer, and continuing his legal studies in Edinburgh in the winter. Uncle John, now 86, was angry that his expense for Thomas's political career had what he called "no adequate return" and was not at all in favour of the part-time work on his estates, believing that a factor should be in permanent residence so as to familiarise himself with all the problems. But he need not have worried. This period of unsettlement in Thomas's career heralded a severe nervous breakdown which he suffered on his withdrawal from politics in 1837. Talking incoherently for 24 hours, he was put into Saughton Hall, Edinburgh, then an asylum. Disturbed about religion, politics and marriage, he suffered a relapse, and died in April 1838 in his 28th year.

Deeply shocked, Uncle John began to wonder when the misfortunes of his family would end. His next great-nephew, William's third son David, born 1811, followed his father in line for the inheritance, but John could only watch this boy's progress with a detached interest, unable to rid himself of the thought that he might also suffer an early death in the sequence of events which was almost assuming the proportions of a Balfour curse. David, after schooling in Edinburgh, studied to be a lawyer, and despite various bouts of illness, qualified as a Writer to the Signet like his other great-uncle and namesake, David Balfour.

But after appearing to be immortal for so long, John Balfour died at his home in Curzon Street on 15 October 1842, in his 92nd year. He was buried in the Balfour vault at St. Luke's Church. Speculation about the extent of his fortune and its disposal was at an end. Henrietta, his widow, was left his two houses, a large lump sum, and an annuity of £3,000. After small legacies, the rest of the fortune went to Captain William Balfour, R.N.. William had been allowed to keep the income from his uncle's Orkney estates that he had managed in his lifetime. He received a gift of £20,000 which was to be divided between the five surviving children of his first marriage. But by this time, William was well past his 60th birthday. When he was 40 he had made a second marriage and had seven more children. His bride then was Mary Margaret Baikie, an Orcadian, supposed at the time of their wedding on 27 January 1823 to be of a "weakly constitution", but, proved so hardy that she survived her husband by 25 years. William had not long to enjoy his status as the 4th laird of Trenaby, nor the great wealth that he had inherited, for he survived his Uncle John by only four years and died in 1846 when he was sixty-five. During his last years he had bought a house in Moray Place, Edinburgh, a farm at Over Gogar, west-south-west of Edinburgh, and a yacht at Leith for sea-going when he felt the need. His son David, at the age of 35, became the new owner of his grandfather's house, Cliffdale, on Shapinsay, the 5th laird of Trenaby, and the inheritor of the Balfour fortune.

One of his main tasks when he returned to Orkney was to try to be a worthy successor to his popular father. He saw to the application of John Balfour's charitable endowment for the founding of the Balfour hospital in Kirkwall in the premises which are now the West End Hotel, a house which had been built in 1824 as a residence for William Richan of Rapness, and purchased in 1845 for use as a hospital within the terms of the John Balfour Trust. The trustees changed its original name from The Orkney Hospital to The Balfour Hospital in memory of its founder. In the 1920s, it moved to its new premises in the Garden Memorial Buildings off Scapa Road.

In 1844, David Balfour married the lady whom his brother Thomas had courted for so many years – Eleanor Alder Edmeston, the niece of his step-mother, Mary Margaret Baikie, and the daughter of the man who had commanded the Orkney garrison during the Napoleonic War. Thin and theological, she shared David's taste for romanticism. But their marriage, though successful, was to be childless.

David saw the wisdom of being a resident laird on his own estate and became Honorary Colonel of the Volunteer Army. These Volunteers at that time had very little military significance, but provided a satisfactory outlet for patriotic feelings. Frances did not live to see a third-generation Colonel appear in the Balfour/Ligonier family, nor to see Cliffdale, with its early sentimental attraction for her, undergo such a transformation which she would not have imagined in her wildest dreams. With a fortune behind them and the vision to use it to lasting effect, David and Eleanor decided to radically transform the house. The best workmanship was required, so they hired David Bryce, the leading architect and designer, to add to its structure in such proportions that it became the "mock-feudal" mansion that is now known as Balfour Castle. Sandwiched between the baronial-type extensions, it keeps the original staircase up which Mary Balfour used to climb when she went to bed.

Bryce's plans and model can be seen in the castle. The model is in the library, built on a base made in part from an old drawing-board, which retains marks of the sealing-wax used to stick paper to the board, and pencil doodles of an urn. Criticism that the new edifice is pretentious were inevitable, but the castle has made an undeniable impact with its imposing view across the water. Of its many impressive rooms, the most striking is the Italian Room. The soft-green gold-flecked wallpaper, chosen by David and Eleanor, is still on its walls. Italian influence had not then permeated the islands as it did during World War II when Italian prisoners-of-war built the unique and wonderful chapel beside the first Churchill Barrier, but it could be said that the influence of Frances Balfour – daughter of a Frenchman, who loved all things French and Italian, can here be seen. Inherited traits are sometimes capable of skipping a generation, and in David Balfour there was every sign that as well as inheriting the business sense of his grandfather Thomas, he was also endowed with the sensitivity and romanticism of his grandmother Frances. John Balfour's wealth made it possible for Eleanor and him to travel to Italy to secure treasures for the furnishing of this superb room – beautiful pictures and artefacts, gold frames complementing the gold-flecked wallpaper, and one of the most exceptional pieces in the room – a marble-topped table, its surface designed in squares, each in a different marble, strategically placed in front of a mirror so that its reflection makes it appear double its size. The other half of the table is said to be in the Vatican. The ornate ceiling, garlanded with the entwined monograms of David and Eleanor, complements the overall design.

A conservatory, or garden-room, still emphasising the Italian look with its inlaid floor, leads into the garden. Cliffdale, with its three storeys, is the core of the castle. Bryce's design proposed two wings for public and guest rooms to the south, and service-quarters to the east. The laird's suite on the first floor has access to the gardens through the conservatory, and the servants' quarters were designed so as not to overlook the main drive. The library and dining-room are oak-panelled, the library having gargoyles at the vertical divisions of the bookcases. The portrait gallery is lined with generations of Balfours, with the Balfour coat of arms carved in wood on the fireplace with two supporting otters. Above this, and to the right, is a portrait of the first Lord Ligonier wearing the sash of the Order of the Bath, and beside it is a woven tapestry picture of him, mounted on a polished wooden stand. It is here that the Ligoniers and the Balfours meet. The Balfour motto, "Forward", was not lost on the young David Balfour.

Along the coast to the east of the castle is the Balfour burial-ground in the old kirkyard. On a windswept April day, the daffodils are in bloom, and it is possible to stand beside memorials to Mary Balfour's aunts, Elizabeth Manson, of whom she was so fond, and Mary Craigie who was her favourite. David and Eleanor rest there side by side. The last descendants of Captain William Balfour, R.N., through his second wife, rest there also.

Before David Balfour reached his last resting place he made another memorable contribution to Orkney life. One of his private pleasures was in the local songs and ballads which he had heard as a child at home, and noted down so as to remember as many of the words and tunes as he could, both for his own enjoyment and for that of the friends whom he and Eleanor entertained in the drawing-room of Balfour Castle. There were many suggestions that he should edit these for publication, but this he did not manage until 1885 when he was in his seventies. His fascinating collection, "Ancient Orkney Melodies", collected by Colonel David Balfour of Balfour, was published by Ballantyne, Hanson & Co., Edinburgh, that year, and was republished by the Orkney Press, Kirkwall, in 1985.

The example of Uncle John and his father William had shown David the importance of being a conscientious land-owner which had involved him also in certain responsibilities as a public figure. Popular and respected, he was awarded the Freedom of the Burgh of Kirkwall on 21 November 1861, when he was 50. This gave him a platform on which to stress the urgent need for proper drains and an unpolluted water supply in the area, recalling the death of his baby brother John ,who had died as a victim of the tainted wells of Kirkwall. But, typically, it took all of ten years, letters, poems, and leading articles in the Press before public opinion was convinced that Colonel Balfour's plan should be implemented. He was elected Provost, and a safe water supply was secured. He found his involvement in public life rewarding, and expressed his thankfulness that "my sphere of duty has been so congenial and to my taste as to amount to a positive pleasure – moving as I have done among the people I love so dearly".

He died in 1887 aged seventy-six, one of the most successful and influential of the Balfour lairds that Orkney has known, fortunate in being endowed with a generous amount of capital and an appealing personality. The Balfours of Trenaby had taken about three generations to acquire the Shapinsay lands and to benefit from the wealth that John Balfour had accrued, and the romantic vision that culminated in Balfour Castle. The slow decline of the Orkney lairds who had been in evidence since the 16th century, was brought about by the consequences of Gladstone's Ballot Act (1872), the Third Reform Act (1884) and the Crofters' Act of 1886. Three generations after David Balfour's death the line of the Orkney lairds was extinct.

David's half-brother, Colonel James William Balfour, first son of his father's second marriage, was the sixth laird of Trenaby. When he died in 1907 he was succeeded as the seventh laird by his only son, William Edward Ligonier Balfour, who died in 1934. As the seventh laird's children were both daughters, Mildred and Doris, there was no direct male heir to follow the long line of Balfours who had contributed so successfully to Orkney life over 200 years.

So the wheel turns, and the unpredictability of life goes on. Frances Ligonier/Balfour, the English society lady, once thought too old a bride to take as her husband the young second son of the laird of Trenaby, and a very unlikely person to fit into the Orkney scene, gave birth to William, the son whose popularity in Orkney didn't come through being an Old Harrovian, or a distinguished

Royal Navy officer, high enough standards in themselves, but because, as the 4th laird, he earned, through his inherited standards of living, the wealth that he and his son had the vision to use for the lasting benefit of the islands.

That his sister Mary, Frances's only daughter, when the wife of a Church of Scotland minister in Edinburgh, wrote two best-selling novels, is another part of this story.

Thomas and Frances

In the late eighteenth century the journey by road from London to Edinburgh took sixty hours by coach, and then Orkney had to be reached by sea. Frances, undeterred, viewed the prospect of her new life as a welcome change from the social whirl of London. That the Orkney countryside seemed open and treeless, with scarcely any road worthy of the name, was of little importance. Her first settled home was on the tiny island of Burray between South Ronaldsay and the Mainland, about four miles long and two and a half miles wide.

Thomas had looked for a house which would please her, and chose the Bu of Burray. The word “bu” was used in Orkney to denote a manor-house or an estate. Originally, this old Norse word referred to a big farm, but later came to mean a large dwelling-house with barns, out-houses and garden. This is how the Bu of Burray looked when Frances first saw it. The half-timbered cottage beside Cobham Park which they had leased after their marriage had been close to her brother and his wife, but after suffering a miscarriage in the spring of 1777, she had been depressed. Life in Orkney presented a fresh challenge early in 1778, when she found herself pregnant again. The splendid stretch of sandy beach on the east of Burray and the three-quarters of a mile of bright sand with the remains of two brochs on the north would make an ideal playground for children.

The people of Burray had not forgotten an earlier laird, Sir James Stewart, who less than forty years earlier appeared before the High Court Justiciary for taking, with the help of three others, Henry Mowat, from his house on Fara with his servant and his cattle, beating him until he bled, carrying him by boat to the island of Flotta, extorting a bill from him for 40 pounds Scots, and eventually forcing him to work at Burray without pay.

Stewart had already murdered Captain James Moodie, R.N., uncle of his old political rival, James Moodie of Melsetter, after a fight in Broad Street, Kirkwall. When Stewart died, unrepentant, in a Hanoverian jail, the Bu of Burray passed to his kinsman, the Earl of Galloway, who later sold it to Sir Laurence Dundas who had appointed Thomas's father, William Balfour, as his factor in Shetland in 1719. Thomas had to negotiate with Sir Laurence for the lease of the Bu. John Sangster had served both the Earl of Galloway and Dundas, and kept it in good order, separating the fields by stone or earth dykes, introducing Dutch white clover and rye-grass among the crops, and supervising the fine herd of cattle. Approaching the Bu by road in the spring down the lane, can be breath-taking. Surrounded by daffodils and bathed in sunshine, no-one would question why Thomas Balfour coveted the place for his English bride. Railings enclose a small front garden with, on each side of the entrance gate, two stone pillars surmounted by stone squirrels. Two large fields facing the house are enclosed by stone dykes and there are stone out-houses, including the old brew-house, the old wash-house and the old water pump which is in the adjacent field. In the bothy, there is a crest high up on the wall which could be the arms of Stewart of Burray showing, in heraldic terms, a fess checky surmounted by a bend engrailed. There is a reproduction of it among the modern coats-of-arms in the library at Graemeshall.

Within a decade of Thomas signing the lease for the Bu, the Statistical Account of Scotland for Orkney and Shetland reported that "in no part of the kingdom can there be seen a richer or more beautiful crop of natural grass mixed with white and red clover. Potatoes, turnips, peas, onions, carrots and cabbages grow on it to perfection". Cattle thrived on the turnips, and rabbits yielded about 2,000 skins in a year. Frances loved it, and entered into every aspect of it with enthusiasm. Necessity made every farmer a fisherman as well as a kelp manufacturer, so on a July morning a man might be seen carrying earth to his dunghill; in the forenoon catching fish; and in the afternoon burning kelp on the shore. The poorest people dug the ground with a bit of iron about 3 inches broad, fixed to the end of a long stick, as fallowing was not used. There was no change of seed, no proper rotation of crops, and the seed oats were never put through a riddle but held up to the wind in the hand or in a creel made of straw. The bere (barley) seeds were put through a riddle, but the small grains were not carefully separated.

Most farmers had a ridge of potatoes which they planted and weeded to get a satisfactory yield. The custom was to sow half a farm with oats which gave only a poor return on account of the weeds. The other half, sown with bere, was well manured with rich farm dung or seaweed, and gave a reasonable crop. Very light ploughs were drawn by four horses, yoked in pairs, and some farmers used harrows with wooden teeth.

Frances found a new sense of contentment. There were no made roads in Burray so few carts were used. Six people with six horses would carry three bolls of bere to the mill. Burray farmers sowed some fields with oats without ploughing at all, except by the noses of their hogs. That way, they were sure of a better crop and fewer weeds.

The shell sand of the Bu Links, ideal for children to play in, and valuable for agriculture, raised an outcry in recent years when a vast amount of it was extracted for the bases of the oil tanks at Flotta and the block works in Kirkwall.

Frances was determined to familiarise herself with the farming calendar – that oats were sown in April, bere in May, and that both were reaped in September/October: that every sheaf, after being cut, was bound and set on end in a triangular position, and if blown over, was set up again, allowing the air to circulate, and then was fastened to other sheaves to prevent it falling again. Now in her mid-thirties, and pregnant, she found that, as the wife of a young husband in an idyllic setting on a remote Scottish island she had a new sense of fulfilment. Burray, with less frost and snow, and a more equal temperature than anywhere else in Scotland, had a better health record than London. The island was so dry, that with only one water-mill, it was rarely possible to grind much of the subtenants' grain. Four kinds of kelp, grown below flood-water mark, were carried on barrows before being spread out to dry, and burnt in a round hole in the earth, lined with stones.

Thomas did not tell Frances that he had asked his mother for financial help when he decided to lease the Bu. Elizabeth Covingtrie, understanding how keen he was to provide a suitable setting for his wife, saw that in financing him she would herself be investing in one of the most valuable farms in Orkney. An inventory of its contents was drawn up by Patrick Fea of Airy in 1747, following the death of the warlike Sir James Stewart whose factor he had been. This revealed an extraordinary collection of broken bits and pieces of improved agricultural implements. There were at least seven English ploughs at a time when few of them were to be found anywhere in Scotland; two-wheeled carts and four-wheeled wagons (when most Orkney parishes had no form of wheeled transport), and, most surprisingly, a turnip-drill plough, ensconced at the Bu of Burray a hundred years before turnips began to be commonly grown as a field-crop. The element of surprise escalated when such things as virginals, billiard tables, backgammon tables and sedan chairs appeared on the list.

Even if most of this treasure-hoard had been dispersed before Thomas took over the lease, he was proud to make Frances mistress of the kind of estate which he considered her due. Closets and rooms which had been inhabited by the Earl of Galloway's family were not unsuitable quarters for the niece of the late Earl Ligonier and the sister of his heir. The dining-room, wine cellar and galleries were under her control. The outside buildings – barns, store-houses, hayloft, cock loft, milk house, brewhouse, washing-house, weaver's house and work-house, were under his.

Thomas has been accused of being more interested in stylish living than in serious farming. Critics saw him as a boy from a good Orkney family whose marriage had gone to his head, who was developing too early a different lifestyle in order to please his older bride. But the critics knew little of his personal problems. If his marriage was to succeed, he must convince Frances that Orkney had its own high standards of living, and bring off the more delicate manoeuvre of getting her accepted by his Orkney relations and friends who had already convinced themselves that she could never become one of them.

Money was his main problem. The year before taking over Burray he was asking Frances's brother, Edward, for financial help, needing more than his mother was prepared to provide. Edward wrote on 9 January 1777 (having seemingly forgotten that a new year had dawned, and that it was now 1778):

Dear Sir
I have received the favour of your letter. You far overate (sic) my poor endeavours to be of service to you, or any part of your family. I wish it was more in my power to prove the esteem and regard I have for you.

Regretting having to turn down Thomas's cry for help, Edward hurried on to the subject of his wife's health, the weather, and his regiment's campaigns which had ended the year with the "Reduction of Fort Washington which clears the Province of New York", and plans for the following year's operation in Canada which was to begin with the attack of Ticonderoga. Only at the end of his letter did he mention his sister's pregnancy:

I find from Mrs Balfour that I am shortly to be an uncle. I wish her a safe escape from this scrape attending marriage, and shall very willingly accept the care of the morals of my nephew by becoming his Godfather. Lady L - joins me in our best wishes for the health and happiness of both of you, and I am, with unfeigned regard,
Ever yours
LIGONIER.

Aware of the shortage of money in his sister's household, Edward renewed his efforts to let Frances's London house. The first tenant, a Mr Cooper, turned out to be what he described as "of the honourable paternity of swindlers", and had only got out of prison a few days earlier when he took possession of "Castel Blanco" (Edward's name for Frances's house). He told Frances what had happened:

I bribed him with six guineas to relinquish possession, and your chateau is now to let. I shall take more care of the next negotiation, and you may be assured, I do not mean that you should suffer

by the late transaction further than being without the Rent I taught you to expect in my last letter. I have no doubt of letting it soon. I shall advertise it. I hope that you continue in perfect health (family circumstances included) and that we shall have a good account of your safe production of that prodigy of wealth and expectations, my niece or nephew. Lady L - sends you her affectionate compliments in which we both join to Mr Balfour and your Orkney friends.
I am ever with real esteem and affection
Yours
LIGONIER.

It was not until October that Edward could report on what seemed a successful negotiation for the tenancy of the house. Writing from Cobham he said:

Mr Porter has offer'd to take the Lease of your house, but he will not pay for your improvements and repairs. I promised to write to you on the subject, and must beg your answer. Lady Ligonier joins me most heartily in our good wishes for your health, and safe delivery. Let us hear from you. I shall ever pay with pleasure the postage that brings me a good account of you. If you produce a boy, I am ready to answer for his future morals under the predicament of Godfather. My compliments to Mr Balfour, and believe me my dear sister
Ever most affectionately yours
LIGONIER.

This time, Lady Ligonier added her own postscript:

If you produce one of the wrong sort I beg I may be godmother and, if I live, will prove one for the affection I bear the mother. Ever my dear Mrs Balfour your affectionate friend
M. LIGONIER.

Frances produced "one of the wrong sort" when she gave birth to a baby girl on 1 November 1778 – All Hallow's Day – a propitious time of arrival for a girl whose later life was to be closely involved with the Christian Church. As a compliment both to Lady Ligonier and to Thomas's youngest sister, the baby was called Mary. Lady Ligonier was delighted to be godmother to the little girl who bore her name. The news reached Cobham in a letter written by Frances 15 days after her daughter's arrival, and by 6 December Edward replied:

My dear Mrs Balfour
I received your letter of the 16 of November and was happy to hear your good state of health, confirmed by yourself. Mr Balfour sent us an account of your safe delivery and of the arrival of a female stranger, which gave us sincere pleasure. I do not know, but it is better than having a boy, as to your comfort, for few mothers see much of their sons after five years of age. Lady L - will ever consider your child as an object of her attachment, for she really loves the mother . . .

Lady Ligonier, fully satisfied, allowed herself expressions of approval in a slightly longer postscript than usual:

My dear Mrs Balfour
I am happy to find you and my God Daughter are well . . . I beg you will take a Harrington care of her and take care of her Beauty. I am surprised you have received no letter of mine. When I get to the town I shall bore you with the novels of London. I am, my Dear Mrs Balfour, in haste, yours most affy.
M. LIGONIER.

A Harrington might have had some connection with the brass farthing made from a patent granted by James I to John, Lord Harrington, in 1613. If so, the "Harrington care" might be seen as the 18th century equivalent of today's savings account.

Edward was now Lieutenant-Colonel. Thomas, after nearly three years in the army, was still an Ensign. Impatience for promotion became more acute now that he was a family man. The cost of the journey from Orkney to London was high, as were his army expenses when he got there. By 1779, when Mary was not a year old, Frances was pregnant again. Thomas had to decide between life with the regiment or life with his family in Orkney. The more he thought about becoming a full-time farming landlord in Orkney, the more appealing it seemed. Frances had settled down, and he was finding pleasure in quarrying stones from the nearby broch for improving his house, building stables and making extra enclosures. But Frances was against him leaving the army and his regimental connections with her brother. She still clung to the conviction, ingrained since childhood, of the important status of an army officer. So, for the time being, Thomas remained in the army. Edward was pleased:

> *I am really glad you do not think at present of quitting the Army, you shall have every indulgence in my power whilst you remain amongst us, and my assistance to procure an eligible manner of retreat for you when you determine to relinquish a Red Coat. I protest, I am as yet uncertain whether or not you are Lieutenant. I hope Mrs Balfour and my niece continue well . . .*

Thomas was promoted Lieutenant on 20 August 1779, with a rise in pay to four shillings and eightpence with three shillings and sixpence subsistence money. Five months later, on 11 January 1780, his first son, John Edward Ligonier Balfour, was born, named to please both Balfour and Ligonier relatives; John, in honour of Thomas's wealthy elder brother, and the gallant Jean-Louis, and Edward, coupled with Ligonier to give satisfaction to Frances's brother who had at last got the nephew he desired.

Mary's hopes of a little sister may have risen when Frances became pregnant the year after John Edward was born. There was concern at Cobham, for Frances was nearing her fortieth birthday. Edward pleaded for the earliest possible news of "her escape from the matrimonial scrape she is now in". "Surely", he wrote to Thomas as the new baby's arrival approached, "she is more reluctant than is common in parting with her burthen. I wish her safely out of it". He felt that she now had enough children "for a modest woman" and hoped she would have no more.

A second son, William, named after his Balfour grandfather, arrived seventeen days before the Christmas of 1781. Edward Ligonier, now a Lieutenant-General, felt in a position to contribute to his sister's growing family, and arranged for a joint payment to be made to her and her husband. He was surprised when Thomas insisted that such a payment should be made solely to Frances, but persuaded himself that Thomas's pay as a Lieutenant must now be sufficient for the family expenditure. He did not think that his brother-in-law was still stinging under his earlier refusal of monetary help when it was asked for, and was hurt when Frances told him after William's birth that his help was no longer required. His disappointment was clear in his letter to her:

> *... I shall obey his and your commands by immediately finishing your future expectations of provision, in short, the bond shall be given up. I have acquitted my conscience in the fruitless attempt I have made to save your annuity, and am more hurt than I can well describe to see you lose your little all, for I consider this transaction in no other view.*

There had been many expenses since Frances received her bequest of £2,000 under the will of Jean-Louis. Thomas reckoned that one way out of domestic and regimental money problems would be to apply for an Adjutancy. An officer holding this position assists superior officers by passing on orders, dealing with correspondence etc. Such an appointment would bring him an increased income without the need to serve with his regiment, so gaining the best of both worlds. With Edward's help, this was arranged, on the strict understanding that it was only a temporary and conditional appointment. But difficulties arose, and nine days after William's birth Edward had to write a strongly-worded letter to Thomas about the Adjutancy:

> *I procured it for you conditionally, and to hold it longer is impossible. If the position of the regiment had admitted of temporising, or that with honor, I cou'd have procured other terms than those applied for, and dispos'd of the Adjutancy in your favour; it would not have been necessary for you to have suggested the idea of advantage for you in the transaction; my wishes to have been of use to you would have been amply sufficient. The Field Officers have frequently remonstrated*

concerning the appointment of Mr Belize being delay'd, and as I can give no account for it, you may guess I appear in colours to them not necessarily concurrent with the idea I must have hitherto deserv'd for Candour and Justice. I see no prospect of any future advantage in your proposal of joining the regiment. What cou'd your presence procure superior to the constant watch I shall have, to seize every opportunity for your service. The expense of your journey must be considerable, your residence with the Regiment even more so, for after so long an absence, you cou'd not decently make a short visit. As to my negotiations at present, there can be none; you have older Lieutenants who indeed are not able to purchase the Capt-Lieutenancy, should it be for sale, but as I see no immediate likelihood of such a vacancy, your presence on that account is by no means necessary, and whilst you have such a vigilant Agent as myself, I think you may rest satisfied. Whenever it falls to your lot to purchase, you sell your Lieutenancy and Ensigncy, but Adjutancys are out of the question unless purchased. I have been perfectly explicit on this subject. If after what I have said, you still wish to join the regiment I have only to add that I shall always be glad to see you...
Lady Ligonier joins me in our affectionate good wishes to my sister, Mrs Balfour, and your fireside. I hope the apples will get safer to Orkney than the pair of stockings which my sister sent for the comfort of my Gouty feet as I have never received them.

On the same day that Edward wrote that letter he was invested at St James's as a Knight of the Bath. Six months later, the Adjutancy question and the Balfours' monetary problems were unexpectedly shelved when he died on 14 June 1782 at the age of 42, before the appointed time for his installation as Knight of the Bath. His honours became extinct. In his will, Frances was left £1,000, with the stipulation that should his estate be less than £3,000 she should have an equal third part. Whatever the residue, she was to have no more than £1,000. Lady Ligonier was the sole executrix. Although Edward was concerned about his wife's delicate state of health, she was to outlive him by twenty-two years, re-marrying five years after his death, on 2 February 1788. Her second husband was Thomas (Noel) 2nd Viscount Wentworth. As Viscountess

Wentworth, the former Lady Ligonier remained a friend to Frances, and retained her interest in Frances's children. She might have played an important part in the shaping of the destiny of her god-daughter had not other events intervened, and she tried to shape the naval career of her nephew William, Mary's younger brother, but without the desired result.

Tom's mother, Elizabeth, wrote to him at Burray after Edward died:

> *I see by my newspaper that Earl Ligonier is dead which must be very heavy on Mrs Balfour for some time, but we are too short-sighted to pronounce what loss it may be to your children. I hope they will be in the care of providence of that being who can work out good from seeming ills.*

The loss was indeed "heavy on Mrs Balfour". When a brother and sister are so close, each relies on the other, and Frances had always relied on Edward.

Five months after his death Thomas wrote to his wealthy brother John, again asking for money. He had already asked him for £200 in the event of Lord Ligonier buying him a Company. John was reluctant to help:

> *Had Lord Ligonier lived you might have got the Company by this means as you got the other two Companies. I have wrote this day to your brother David to remit £100 of my money to you. Be assured there is not a single shilling of that money my own, and you must lay your accounts to pay me at Lammas next.*

With three young children, Frances did not get to London for Edward's funeral. Thomas went, hoping that Lady Ligonier would help in what was now his firm determination to leave the army. Relieved of his former obligations to Edward as his Colonel and brother-in-law, he now saw his way clear to take up farming in Orkney if he could quit the army without discredit to himself or upsetting Frances.

The first time that he called on Lady Ligonier after Edward's funeral she was too upset to see him but invited him to call the following morning. Her affection for him and Frances led her to write on Thomas's behalf to Lord Pembroke, one of the Generals under old Field-Marshal John Ligonier, asking for his help in getting an honourable acquittal for Thomas from the army. She sent Thomas the news in October 1782:

> *Dear Sir*
> *I have just received a letter from Lord Pembroke who has been so very friendly to me, and the memory of his valuable friend, to have exerted his interest with the Commander-in-Chief, and procured leave, contrary to his resolutions, for you to sell. I cou'd not deny myself the satisfaction of communicating this information as soon as I received it.*

This, and other business, kept Thomas in London until late November. On each occasion that he visited Mary Ligonier he was invited to eat mutton with her at five o'clock, mutton being the menu at what was a fashionable time for dinner in the London of the day. With the sale of his commission and the loan from his brother John, he now found himself in a position to consider his own and his family's future. By 1784, when his children were aged five, four and three, the prospect of buying a property rather than leasing one took root in his mind. He was strongly attracted to the Shapinsay property of Sound at Elwick, with its ruined mansion house which had formerly been the property of the Buchanans of Sound, before being passed to the Jacobite supporter, James Fea of Clestrain, and then, after being burnt down by the Royal Navy during the Jacobite Rebellion, to the Chamberlain of Orkney, Andrew Ross. Elizabeth Covingtrie, seeing this as another interesting property, again came to her son's rescue and bought it in the summer of 1784, selling it to him for the considerably reduced price of £1,250 so that he could take possession on 1 October that year.

Elwick (or Elswick) lay in an attractive setting to the south-west of Shapinsay island with a bay opening towards Kirkwall, sheltered by the small green islet of Eller-Holm. It had a fine beach with plenty of fresh water for the young Balfours to enjoy, and one of the best harbours in Orkney. Here the young Mary Balfour spent her childhood and youth, nurtured by her mother in the rudiments of music and dancing, and discovering that there were such languages as French and Italian. Frances planned early that her daughter would be equipped with the necessary ingredients for entrance into London society when she came of age.

Thomas came into farming at a propitious time. A new attitude towards agriculture was beginning to appear in Orkney. One of the leaders of this revolution was Sir John Sinclair from Thurso, a national authority on the subject, and the driving force behind the compilation of the Old Statistical Account by parish ministers who surveyed their parishes on lines laid down by him. His absorption was mainly with planning, but collecting facts was also of prime importance and directed towards the improvement of the rural economy. It was an advantage for Thomas that Sir John Sinclair was his friend. From him he learnt much that was valuable when he began to work the Shapinsay land. Sinclair had discovered that although the larger proprietors in Orkney were absorbing smaller places, there were still too many holdings which were so small that the tenants could not make a reasonable living. This made them frustrated, lazy and unambitious. He saw that grass was the crop best suited to the Orkney environment. Many Orcadians were aware of this, but their low subsistence level made it necessary for them to grow crops for human consumption rather than for cattle. Thomas's initial attempts at growing grass were not successful – his experiments with the rotation of crops were better. He cleared the south-west corner of the island of cottars and set about the administration of his estate. He was now in the work of his choice, temporarily at least, unhampered by financial worries. He turned his thoughts towards improving methods for administering the estate, developing a successful theory that if he introduced the system of a farming ladder, an active farmer could progress from a small holding to a larger one. Run-rig (strip cultivation) was still practised, but some of the larger proprietors began to prefer to enclose and consolidate their holdings. Thomas increased his arable acreage from 700 to 6,000 acres in farms laid out systematically in 10-acre fields. By concentrating on the well-being and better conditions of the farmers, he made it possible for them to produce larger families and so contribute to a much-needed increase in the local population. In 1755, when he was 33, the population of Shapinsay was 642; by 1790, when the numbers rose to 730, the increase was due, according to Rev. George Barry, to the residence of one man – Thomas Balfour. Although Barry's definitive work, *The History of the Orkney Islands,* was not published until about twenty years after Thomas took possession of the Shapinsay estate, it included a mention of individual achievement of note such as the work of Thomas Balfour at Elwick:

> *Previous to his purchase, nothing was to be seen over its whole extent but a dreary waste, interspersed with arable land ill-cultivated, a few miserable hovels scattered thinly over its surface, under the name of farm houses or cottages, which were not fit to shelter from the rigours of the climate a few ragged inhabitants, dirty through indolence, lean with hunger, and torpid by despair. Every thing on this estate now happily wears a very different and more pleasant aspect. An elegant house has been built, and an extensive garden laid out; the lands are substantially enclosed, and judiciously cultivated with the English plough; many barren fields are, by cultivation made fertile; summer fallowing, with a change of seed and rotation of crops is introduced with good effect; and the soil which formerly bore with reluctance coarse grass, and scanty heather and puny oats and bear (bere), now cheerfully produces oats, rye, barley, pease, wheat, potatoes, clover and turnips, in considerable quantity and of a good quality. Together with these improvements, the same gentleman has erected a village by the side of the harbour at Elwick, in which he has placed, joiners, carpenters, weavers, tailors shoemakers, coopers, and labourers of various sorts, furnished them with work sufficient to employ them; and thus enabled them from the fruits of their industry to marry early, and to produce numerous families. In short, Cliffdale, which is the name of this gentleman's seat, taken in conjunction with its appendages, exhibits to the eye of a stranger coming from the sea, or from Kirkwall, rather the appearance of a neat little villa in the vicinity of some opulent city, than of a gentleman's house recently raised in a remote part of the kingdom.*

Basically, Cliffdale was a plain building on three floors with nothing over-elaborate in its design. It fitted well into the surrounding landscape. Working hard, Thomas became an active and knowledgable laird, gaining popularity for being resident on his estate which was not always the practice on the larger Orkney properties at that time. George Barry underlined the advantage to the tenants of a residential laird:

> *Among the people in a country parish whose farms are small and whose tacks (leases) are only verbal, the residence of heritors, if they be men of sense and virtue, is of the greatest advantage. They silence disputes, and terminate any differences which may arise by their authority; they set an example of industry, and by their smiles or their frowns, not only distinguish the deserving from the worthless, but reward the one, while they punish the other.*

Experiments in crossing native sheep with Southdowns, renowned for their lambing performance, were made on the Balfour estate. Kelp gave Thomas four times the amount of profit that he was getting from the land. Kelp and linen work competed with agriculture work for labour, and farmers had to pay their men £2 -£3 as well as their keep from August to June. For the rest of the summer they burned kelp and made another £1, with their keep.

Five hundred years before Thomas took over Elwick, the Norwegian king, Haakon Haakonsson, had, at the end of July 1263, led an expedition to Shetland and sailed his fleet to Orkney where he anchored in Elwick Bay. Mindful of this historical event, Thomas, taking his cue from those Vikings of old, kept 20 boats in Elwick harbour including four brigs and four sloops with fifty sailors to man them.

The young Balfour children grew up happily in these surroundings. But with the passage of childhood, more formal education had to be considered. The Union of the Parliaments in 1707 initiated changes in the Scottish way of life. Wealthy Scottish lairds found themselves moving in English social circles, emulating those of their countrymen who worked for the Government and were already involved. Horizons were widening. Frances, an

Englishwoman at heart, viewed this new development with keen interest. Her appreciation of the English educational system need no longer be viewed as suspect from the Scottish point of view. Thomas became aware of the rising importance of an English public school education, emphasised when there was a dramatic increase in the number of Scots who decided that English public schools were the right places for their sons. Harrow, rather than Eton was the preferred choice of those who lived north of the border, so Thomas and Frances decided to enter their two sons for this seat of education which was becoming increasingly popular for upper-class Scottish boys. It was younger by 85 years than Kirkwall Grammar School. "Good Queen Bess" had granted the charter to John Lyon to found a Free Grammar School at Harrow in 1572. Its showplace, the Jacobean Old Schools, has a wing, completed in 1615, which contains the original form room in which the Headmaster used to perch at the North End with his Usher at the South, with the boys on the benches in between. Known as the Fourth Form Room, this atmospheric oak-panelled chamber is covered with names of former illustrious pupils such as Byron, Peel, Trollope, and Sheridan. So Harrow, with its strong links with aristocratic and old landed families, was chosen by Thomas and Frances for the education of their sons.

No stones were left unturned to secure their entrance, so a suitable tutor must be found. Schoolmastering was often a prelude to the ministry, and the Balfour's choice fell on a young theology student from Edinburgh, Alexander Brunton, who was entrusted with the task of bringing John Edward and William to the required educational standard. Concentrating on the means to the end, neither Thomas nor Frances could foresee what far-reaching results the presence of the young minister from Edinburgh within their household would have. With the future of their sons in mind, they failed to discern what an unsettling effect that daily contact with a personable young man was having on their teenage daughter.

Success as a landowner gave Thomas a status which increased when his sons passed into Harrow. The prestige of his brother John, Member of Parliament for Orkney, gave added status to the boys. John took an avuncular interest in the progress of his nephews, monitoring their progress with the reward of receiving from them the attention due to a celebrated uncle. In the autumn term of 1793, his elder nephew, Edward, wrote to him from Harrow:

But half an hour a day is not employed at Latin. Tell my father that there can be no benefit derived from learning to write or dance here as the dancing master stays two hours at the time and comes once a week, so there can be nothing got from him, and as to the writing master, he indeed attends every morning but only remains a few minutes with us. But as to the Latin business, we are always at work. I may say, and safely so, that I have learned more since I came here than I used to learn in twice the time at Mr. Macfarlan's.

Thomas had had a letter in the Spring Term of 1792 in reply to his letter asking, with typical paternal concern, about progress. Edward did his best to supply the need:

I still keep the same place in my class as before, and William is second in his. When you wrote me you told me to tell you what time we were at school. Eight hours in the day, and during that time we do Ovid by turns, that is, the class I am in. On Sunday we do Latin testament. We are very well liked by everyone of the boys, but one is an Indian who is hated by all the boys for his tyranny and blackgardly manner. Give my love to all my friends and relations in O. I can say no more at present but that I have had about a dozen bathes since Cristmas (sic) holidays, and that I am

Your dutiful son
John Ed Lr Balfour
Walthamstow, 24th April 1792.

Pressure from Frances could have made Thomas "strain every nerve" to raise a regiment of Fencibles in Orkney. The Army Lists of 1795 record that as from 20 April 1793, the Orkney Fencibles were formed with Thomas Balfour as their Major – the 8th regiment of its kind to be raised in Scotland. From January 1794, it was called The Orkney and Shetland Fencibles. Thomas worked hard to raise recruits, sending recruiting parties into every Orkney island as well as to the Highlands, and crossed the ferry himself to Caithness to drum up extra men. Most of the men were Orcadians. Privates received 1/- a day, corporals 1/2d, and sergeants 1/6d. Fencible Units came under full military law and were used in the war against revolutionary France. Thomas chose the colours of his former regiment, the 9th Foot, for their uniform – a black cocked hat, a scarlet coat faced with yellow, and a white cross-belt, white pantaloons and black gaiters. The regimental march, composed by himself, still survives.

Serving at home, and at Berwick-on-Tweed, the Orkney Fencibles and their officers gained a reputation for the amount of liquor they could put away. Between 30 September and 4 November 1797, Major James Moodie and nine other officers, when stationed at Berwick-on-Tweed, got through 103 bottles of wine and 372 gills of gin. The wine cost 2/6d a bottle and the gin 1d a gill. Brandy and claret would have been unobtainable from France at that time, so gin or port or sherry were the substitutes. The most abstemious of the party in the autumn of 1797 was a young Ensign who only consumed liquor to the value of 7/6d.

But the raising of this regiment was not universally approved. An Orkney lady complained that the raising of the Fencibles was "as bad a thing as could be done in the locality". Orkney men who were trying to find recruits for the Navy were angry too, for their task was being made more difficult by the Fencibles. Eventually, in December 1797, the Orkney and Shetland Fencibles were disbanded.

Another Fencible Regiment was formed in 1794 – The North Lowland Fencible Regiment. Thomas saw in it the chance of promotion to the army rank most desired for him by Frances, and joined it as Colonel as from 30 October 1794. The list of officers included the name of Captain John E. Ligonier Balfour, Thomas's elder son. In the early months of 1794 an army career was being mapped out for this young man. A lively, good-natured boy, quixotic, with something of his Aunt Mary's talent for poetry and short stories, he, at fourteen, went along with the plans for his career which his father, his uncle John, and his aunt, Lady Wentworth, were putting into motion. Lady Wentworth wanted to use her influence with Lord Amherst for her nephew's advancement, but was restrained by his uncle John who, cautious as ever, knew that any application for army entrance would require a birth certificate to prove that the applicant was sixteen – the minimum age required for recruitment at officer status.

So Uncle John suggested that Edward should first become an Ensign in the Fencibles where no questions would be asked, and from there be transferred to the regimental army – a necessary procedure if he wished to get a Lieutenancy. By the October of 1794, John Balfour had arranged with Colonel Forbes for his nephew to become a Lieutenant in the 105th Regiment, the Colonel promising to give him "as much indulgence as shall be in my power in respect of leave of absence" without any firm guarantee.

The young trainee minister, Alexander Brunton, having successfully fulfilled his task of tutoring the Balfour boys for Harrow, was discovering in Orkney some useful practical experience for his ministerial work. Military chaplaincy was an unusual appointment for so young a man, but Thomas had been impressed by the successful tutoring of his sons and saw him as the right man for the position of Chaplain to the Fencible Regiment. He also mentioned his confidence in Alexander Brunton to Rev. George Barry, the minister of Shapinsay Church, who, harassed by all the necessary research for his important book on *The History of the Orkney Islands*, was unable to give as much time to his parish work as was needed, especially to the preparation of his Sunday sermons.

So, newly licensed by the Presbytery of Linlithgow at the age of twenty-four, Mr Brunton was invited in the summer of 1796 to take the service at Shapinsay Church – the church attended by Thomas Balfour and his family. He chose as his text "The Kingdom of God is within you". The Shapinsay folk had too long been starved of the thought-provoking sermons which they needed, and this young man, by his earnest delivery, gave a welcome answer to their needs. If they hoped that he would remain in their midst, such a hope was to be short-lived. Only a year later they learnt with disappointment that on 28 September 1797, he had been ordained to Bolton near to Haddington in East Lothian.

But the Orkney Islands had not heard the last of him by any means.

Mary and Alexander

Kirkwall Grammar School had been Orkney's centre of education since James III granted the 1486 charter to the town. It supplied schooling when there were few other centres of education in the islands. Parish reports from 1627 reveal a complete absence of schools outside Kirkwall. At the end of the 18th century there were only a few parochial schools.

But for the changes brought about by the Union of the Parliaments, Thomas and Frances would probably have sent their children to the Kirkwall Grammar School which Thomas's father and grandfather had attended. But as they were entering their sons for Harrow, the education of their daughter was becoming a matter of growing importance. In the late 18th century, public schools for girls in England had not come into the same prominence as those for boys. Edinburgh was nearer home, a city that Thomas knew well from his time at the University. His brother David was a Writer to the Signet there, and his sister Margaret lived there alone and would welcome her young niece. And Alexander Brunton was training for his degree in Classics and Theology in Edinburgh.

Parish Schools were in Liberton, Cramond and Colinton, but had the Balfours wished a Parish School for Mary there were plenty in Orkney. Eventually they chose one of the Edinburgh Private Schools which were advertised as teaching mathematics, languages, cookery . . . and dancing. Some Orkney girls had been at school in the city as early as 1749. Eighteenth century Edinburgh courses were attractive with their practical variety of subjects. A Mrs McIver taught in the Peebles Wynd, and from 1779-1786 in

Stevenlaw's Close, offering lessons in cooking, preserving and pickling for 15/- a quarter.

Mary's second novel *Discipline,* (Chapter II) gives a clue to the kind of school which she attended. Ellen, the problem-child, and later the heroine of the novel, is sent to a "fashionable boarding-school" which her father hopes will remedy her intractable behaviour after the death of her mother:

> *I was conveyed to - House, then one of the most polite seminars of the metropolis . . . My father, who did not pique himself with the mysteries of education, gave no instructions in regard to mine, except that expense should not be spared on it; and he certainly never found reason to complain that this injunction was neglected. For my own part, I submitted, without opposition, to the change in my situation. The prospect of obtaining companions of my own age reconciled me to quitting the paternal roof, which I had late found a melancholy abode.*

Ellen's comments in *Discipline* about the - House curriculum are sufficient to confirm that Mary was describing her own school which offered a continuation of the early language tuition which she had received from her mother:

> *We were taught the French and Italian languages, but, in as far as was compatible with these acquisitions, we remained in ignorance of the accurate science, or elegant literature to which they might have introduced us. We learnt to draw landscape, but, secluded from the fair originals of nature, we gained not one idea from the art, except such as was purely mechanical . . .*

More from the pages of *Discipline* give evidence that - House was indeed Mary's Edinburgh school, especially Ellen's remark that the school's advertisements stressed that the utmost attention should be paid to the morals of the pupils. If Mary, in her seven years of education there, had, with her fellow-pupils, to repeat a page of the Catechism every Sunday afternoon before "meditating at eventide in the Park", this would have contributed to her later philosophy of life, leading her to the realisation of the importance of morals, as well as the need to impart such a philosophy to the world. But - House, in *Discipline,* deals also with the less sober facts of life – the art of wearing clothes fashionably – "arranging our decorations with grace and effect" – an undeniable advantage to any young girl's entrance into what was, even then, a very competitive world.

So autobiographical do some of the early pages in *Discipline* seem, that Mary may have made Ellen her mouthpiece when she left school at the end of seven years of "laborious and expensive trifling" with only one real accomplishment – music. Mary was not like Ellen in wishing to excel in it in order to do better than one of her schoolfriends who was forever provoking her, she was sufficiently dedicated to practise seven hours a day to attain the standard for which she was to be praised long after her schooldays were over. If she left school in her sixteenth year, it sets the date of 1795, a few months after she wrote a letter from her aunt Margaret's house in Edinburgh to her Aunt Craigie in Orkney – the first of her letters known to have survived:

Edinburgh February 4th 1795

My Dear Mrs Craigie

I have the pleasure to inform you that my Aunt has been visibly better these eight days. Her reachings are much less frequent and her spirits much better: while I write she is lying on a sopha singing. Its no very lang sin syne. - The intense cold of the weather at present is greatly against her, as it precludes all possibility of her going out an airing. -Dr Wardrop, whose very looks must be salutary to the sick, attends her every day, and Dr Monro who is the principal physician in the town comes once a week. The cold here is more intense than anything I ever felt. I am credibly informed that on the night of Friday last a thermometer on a level with the snow and with an eastern exposure fell 5 below 0. My Father is still in London as it is impossible to travel from thence in a carriage. He has had a bad cold but is now quite recover'd. We expect him down as soon as the roads are passable. Lady Charlotte Hope has been to see us and I have dined at her house. She is rather pretty, very genteel and has a modesty and sweetness in her manners and appearance which are very taking to a stranger. - We see Mr and Mrs Balfour every day. Their son George is in very bad health. I am much afraid they will lose him. He looks extremely ill and has a bad cough, poor thing, his mind is weaken'd with his body and he is much more childish than his sister. - There are a great many little birds sitting in the window picking the crumbs I have laid out for them. I am told there are hundreds found in the fields, frozen or starved to death. Mr Du Monti is just come so I must conclude by desiring my best respects to Mr Craigie and grandmama and subscribing myself my Dear Mrs Craigie

Your Affectionate Niece

M. BALFOUR.

Postage services to Orkney had been steadily improving since 1741, when bags of mail were made up in Edinburgh for despatch to the islands, and they improved even more after the Kirkwall post office was established in 1747. But bad weather was still a hazard, delaying deliveries. Mary experienced this at the end of February 1795, when, after waiting four weeks for a reply from Aunt Craigie, she wrote again:

I am sorry that I cannot say that my Aunt is anything better than when we came here; indeed she has so many sudden changes that it is impossible to say one day how she will be the next. I would fain hope the Dr thinks her in little or no immediate danger. My father, who left us three days ago for Orkney, will be able to inform you more particularly of my aunt's situation so that I shall say nothing more of it but that she is no longer troubled with those violent sweats which till lately distressed her exceedingly. I am afraid Mama confines herself too much to the house, for she had hardly cross'd the threshold above once or twice since she came to Edinburgh. Papa is getting his picture done by the same hand that painted Uncle David. I have seen it and the likeness is striking. The weather which has long been intensely cold is now improving and there has been a gentle thaw for a few days. Fine weather will be greatly in my Aunt's favour as she will then take an airing every day. Mrs Balfour has lately lost a brother who had long been deranged by a paralytic stroke and who in consequence of another has been confined to bed these two years.

Mary kept up an interest in her father's estate which had been her only other home. Once she relayed a message about it to Aunt Craigie from her mother, then in Edinburgh:

Mama requests the favour of you if you can gather from papa how many milk cattle he wou'd have at Sound (in case they amount to twenty) to engage Marabel Corstan for the next term and likewise to hint to my father that as there will be nobody at home through the spring it wou'd be proper to make a division of the grass, distinguishing what is for the cows from that intended for other cattle; otherwise it will be the cause of continual disputes between the Grieve of the Day. Mamma will write you next post and hopes papa will have reach'd you before that time. She sent your stays by John Sargeson and your gown by Isabel Tait. She hopes you will get them safe. Present my best respects to Mrs Manson, Mr Craigie and Grandmama, and believe me to be, dear aunt,

Your Affectionate Niece
M. BALFOUR.

The painter of the portraits of "Uncle David" and "Papa" was Henry Raeburn, once a goldsmith's apprentice in Parliament Close, Edinburgh. David Wilkie, writing from Madrid where he had been studying Velasquez, said:

There is much resemblance between him and some of the chiefs of the English School; but of all, Raeburn resembles him most, in whose square touch in heads, hands, and accessories I see the very counterpart of Velasquez.

As the material prosperity of Scotland developed, so there emerged many well-to-do citizens, agriculturalists, and merchants, who were affluent long before middle-age. Literature and Science kept pace with this development, and the 18th-19th century did not pass without its pictorial record. Mary's father, and her Uncle David, were just two of these important citizens who were painted by Raeburn in his studio at 32, York Place, where he walked every morning to be ready for his first sitter at nine. He rarely had less than three or four sitters a day, giving an hour and a half to each. When Thomas sat for his portrait he was placed on a pedestal, and gazed at by a pair of great dark eyes. Once Raeburn got the idea of his sitter, he would rush up to the canvas, not looking at the subject, and put down what he had recorded in his "inner eye". Then he would stand back, look again, and record what he saw. He was knighted by George IV at Hopetoun House and created His Majesty's Limner for Scotland.

Perhaps during her schooldays in Edinburgh, Mary saw something of Alexander Brunton, and began to experience some romantic feelings about him. Frances, with a mother's intuition, became uneasy. The last thing she wanted for her daughter was that she should marry someone with no social standing and little money. Taking matters into her own hands, she whisked Mary back to Orkney as soon as her schooldays were over and saw to it that she was fully occupied looking after father, and helping in the domestic arrangements at Cliffdale for the next four years.

But when Alexander Brunton was invited to preach in Shapinsay Church the year after Mary left school, Frances's anxiety increased.

Parents will often go to endless trouble to steer their offspring away from associations which they consider unsuitable. Frances, with mounting concern, felt that unless she took firm action, Mary would present her with a ministerial son-in-law with a ridiculously small stipend, and no social standing, an idea which she did not care for at all.

When the friendship appeared to be becoming closer, she took the step of banishing Mary to the small island of Gairsay, between Shapinsay and Rousay. Stunned and unhappy, it was small consolation to Mary that Gairsay had once been the stronghold of the great Viking pirate chief, Sweyn Asleifsson of Langskaill, that the foundations of his magnificent sixty-foot drinking-hall were believed to be under the house, and that the mansion with its bowling green and sunken garden was a reconstruction of the late

16th-century house by Sir William Craigie, M.P., one of the most powerful and astute Orcadians of his century.

Frances cleverly arranged this so that it would be looked on as a little holiday for Mary with the affluent Craigies. Sir William Craigie's motto *Timor Omnis Abest* - Dread Nought, was above the arched gateway at Langskaill which may have given Mary some courage and hope.

Frances did not intend this to be a permanent arrangement. Emphasising to her sister-in-law, Viscountess Wentworth, Mary's godmother, how remote an area Orkney was for a young girl of Mary's age – so little social life – nothing to compare with London, she felt confident that Lady Wentworth, childless from two marriages, and always generous, would lose no time in sending an invitation to her goddaughter to come and stay with her in London, enjoying the thought of introducing her niece into London society. Mary Balfour would be well qualified to mingle there as the grand-daughter of a Colonel and the great-niece of a former Field-Marshal and Commander-in-Chief of the British Army.

But when this proposition of a new and exciting life among the smart set of London was presented to her, Mary was faced with an appalling dilemma. Alexander Brunton had asked her to marry him.

It was an impossible situation for a nineteen-year-old girl. Torn by the conflict of having to refuse the generous offer of the godmother whom she really loved, and of displeasing and shocking her mother with the news of her engagement, she knew that her mind was irrevocably made up. The prospect of a quiet life in a Scottish country manse held far more attraction for her than all the bright lights of London.

Gairsay was, then as now, only accessible by boat from the mainland which ferries supplies and passengers across to the small harbour. A hundred years after Mary's enforced stay there, the population was only 33, so any plans she may have made for her escape were not likely to be spoilt by the spread of idle gossip. It was the end of 1798 when she found herself in what could almost be described as an episode in a fairy tale – the marooned princess with no way of communicating with her lover – no telephone, and only the sort of postal service which could not be relied upon for delivery the following day. She was like Rapunzel, imprisoned in a seemingly unassailable fortress. But Alexander Brunton was not a young man to be thwarted. Somehow he managed to arrange for Mary to give him a pre-arranged signal from the island, and he then, as chivalrous as the proverbial knight in shining armour, would secretly row over in a small boat, probably from the mainland, and whisk her away. An operation, no less romantic for being undertaken in the sometimes fickle late autumn weather. But fortune favoured him and he rescued his girl.

On 4 December 1798, five weeks after her 20th birthday, they were married. In the Edinburgh Register of Marriages, Rev. Alexander Brunton is described as of Bolton Parish, and Mary, daughter of Colonel Balfeur (sic) of Cliffdale, Orkney, as of St Andrew's Parish, an Orkney parish, the minister of which, in 1843, was one of the dissidents who left the Established Church to form the Free Church.

Mary was prepared for a storm to break after her wedding, but was not prepared for its ferocity. Frances, enraged that her daughter had dismissed any chance of marriage with one of the highly-connected members of London society, was having little support from Thomas in her protestations. He was in London at the time of the crisis and very ill. She did not know that he had a mistress, Mrs Mary Clifford, three months pregnant by him. Frantically seeking some form of sympathy, Frances poured out her hurt feelings in letters to her Orkney sisters-in-law, Elizabeth Manson and Mary Craigie. But these made little impact as both were very busy wives with little time to come back with expected indignation at their niece's marriage. Alexander Brunton, to them, seemed a very nice young man.

Frances had inherited an excitable temperament from her French father. Staying with her brother-in-law David Balfour and his family in Hanover Street, Edinburgh, at the time of the wedding, she expected him to rise to her support, and was deflated when, with his less volatile Scottish temperament, he mildly viewed his niece's behaviour as "imprudent and undutiful". So another letter went to Elizabeth Manson – a terrible, despairing outburst from a woman approaching the age of sixty who was seeing her family gradually slipping away, and leaving her alone. John Edward, her eldest son, was a Captain in the 9th Foot, her late brother's regiment, which to her was a matter of pride and satisfaction but tinged with more than a little apprehension that he might meet his death in battle as her father had done. William, her younger son, was in the Navy, and she suspected that she had already lost Thomas, either to his ladyfriend, or because he was already mortally ill. In Mary she had visualised the enjoyment of the rewarding mutual companionship which mother and daughter can share. Frances had seen this as sharing the delights of London life. Suddenly, all such hope had vanished and the support she had expected from her husband's Orkney family had not come. Suddenly, she began to feel very much alone.

Such a marriage as Mary's did not fail to create gossip and make tongues wag. An Orcadian lady, Mary Fraser, living in the Morningside district of Edinburgh during the winter of 1798-99, wrote to her cousin, Jeany McKinlay, in Kirkwall:

> *I am sure you would be surprised to hear of Miss Mary Balfour's marriage with Brunton, her father and mother are not like to be reconciled to it. I really think there is no wonder – for however good and clever he might be, he certainly was not a match for her. She is situated very near a friend of ours, in the country, who tells me, that she is a pleasant woman, and goes about visiting her neighbours in a cart, as happily as she used to do in her Father's carriage. Whatever she may feel it shows her wisdom to appear contented since it was entirely her own doing.*

Mary was not insensitive to her mother's reaction. Anxious to ease the situation and make her peace with the Orkney aunts of whom she was very fond, she sought some reassurance in a letter written to Elizabeth Manson six weeks after her wedding:

> *St James's Square*
> *January 18th 1799.*
>
> *My dear Aunt,*
> *It is natural for one who is conscious of error, and wou'd ask indulgence, to collect for their support every conciliating circumstance – With this view, I have delay'd writing to you till I can now do it under my father's roof and under the immediate*

protection of my natural friends. Among these, may I still venture to class you? I have received much kindness from you and shou'd be truly sorry that any part of my conduct occasion'd your lasting displeasure. We remain here I believe but for a short time – Our house is finish'd and but for the attending damp we might now inhabit it – but we must necessarily leave town before it is ready for us, that the furniture may be put up, and that we may lay out the little spot that is to supply us with many of the necessities of life. – For these purposes we are to occupy a furnished house near our own and lent us by an acquaintance or rather friend of Mrs Brunton's during her stay in town for the winter season. Once settled there the world for me may bustle in vain. I shall join in the bustle no more. – There is an excellent neighbourhood in which Mr Brunton is much beloved. But where he is known and not beloved -

Mama bids me assure you that you do her an injustice if you think she has not written for she has sent you two letters by post and one by ship. – Mr Brunton and she join me in best compliments to you and Mr Manson. Allow me to subscribe myself

Your affectionate Niece
MARY BRUNTON

Part of Frances's tragedy was that for the last fourteen years of her life, she was consumed with bitterness and suspicion which harassed even her closest friends. She was able to cope when things went right, but felt hopeless and alone when they went wrong.

Mary was enchanted with her new home. Any doubts about the rightness of her decision to marry Alexander, or "Mr B" as she liked to call him, were soon dispersed. Bounded by Haddington, Yester, Humbie and Saltoun, Alexander's parish in East Lothian was situated in quiet countryside. The stone-built manse stood close to the church with a small front garden and a larger back garden with apple trees and the mill-lade off the Coalston Water running gently at the foot of the field beyond the garden wall. Here was her dreamed-of escape from the bustle of the world. Here Mr B involved himself in parish work and discovered that he could leave matters of church policy to others, as his predecessors had done before him.

Of the 2,300 acre parish, 170 acres were planted, and the soil was fertile. The minister's stipend (to the amazement of his mother-in-law) was paid in bolls of wheat, bolls of bear (barley) and bolls of oats, the boll being a dry measure of weight which varied with the commodity and the locality. A boll of meal could equal 140lbs (approx. 63.5kg). The minister also received a few pounds sterling which would include such things as Vicarage Tithes and Communion Elements, and the rent of a glebe of about 4 acres. The glebe was the portion of land traditionally assigned to a parish minister in addition to his stipend. A glebe of over 6 acres could be let for about £25. The minister could also receive "grass-maill" – a rent for pasturage which could bring in about £20 Scotch. The Scotch pound (or pund) was worth one-twelfth of the English pound. Separate currencies were abolished by the 1707 Act of Union, but calculations were still made on the basis of the Scots system until the late 18th century.

Bolton was a comparatively small village. The population in the Bruntons' time was between 235 and 252. There was a smithy close to the manse and one of Mary's favourite walks was down the lane between the smithy and the manse to the rustic bridge over the river with its overhanging trees where she would stand and watch the trout stream with its quiet and gentle beauty, and enjoy the charm of the large thatched dovecote (or doocot) nearby. There was a corn mill, a barley mill, and a school behind the church, which might have an average of 72 pupils in the winter months. The salary of the schoolmaster was 100 Scots pounds. A hundred years before the Bruntons came to Bolton the schoolmaster had been a man called Ninian Miln who was dismissed for neglect of the school, for "scandalous tippling and drinking" and not filling up the registers.

Alexander had 54 families under his care, 106 males and 129 females. The farms were widely-spaced. There were about 230 acres in oats in the area. Not many potatoes or turnips were grown – turnips were looked on as a delicacy and sometimes served as a dessert. A ploughman could earn £14 a year. Tenants had to carry their own coal, and their thirlage to the mills.

He performed the usual round of duties – baptisms, marriages and funerals. In 1783, Bolton Kirk decided that a "new fashionable hearse" should be purchased out of the funds of the poor. Bought in November of the same year at a cost of £37.14s., it was used to bring the body of the 10th Lord Blantyre from Bath, Somerset, for burial, and was in regular use for all the funerals that Alexander had to conduct in Bolton. It is believed to be the oldest surviving road vehicle in Scotland.

Anyone who went to their grave in it was transported in state. The roof design was influenced by the contemporary taste in Chinese/Chippendale furnishings. Suspended by leather straps at the front and back on large upright supports, it was free to sway from side to side and end to end. The sides were decorated with a skull, the words "Memento Mori" (remember that you must die), an hour-glass with the inscription "Hora Fugit" (the hour flies), and canary-coloured tears two inches long. In the front, a narrow roofed extension of the body of the hearse was used for food for the horses, ropes for lowering the remains into the grave, and nails and a hammer in case of accidents. The box also served as a seat for the driver.

It carried the poor as well as the nobility. When the retired schoolmaster of Athelstaneford, Naesmith Simpson, died, the hearse took his body from Haddington to Lyne in Peebles-shire with the instructions that there were to be 4 horses, 2 attendants, mourning coaches, and a jar of 2 gallons of whisky to be provided for refreshment on the road and at the graveside. The mourners and the driver were recommended to stop and refresh themselves at every public-house they came to – both going to, and on return from the grave. Not surprisingly, the hearse did not return to Haddington until two days after the funeral.

It achieved lasting fame by taking Agnes Brown, mother of Robert Burns, to her grave in Bolton Kirkyard in 1820, and her son Gilbert, and her daughter Annabella, there when they died. It has been in the Royal Scottish Museum in Edinburgh since 1932.

Gilbert Burns came to Bolton at the end of the Bruntons' time as farm manager to Mrs Dunlop at Morham West Mains who had been a friend of his brother Robert, the poet. When he became factor to Lord Blantyre in 1804, and moved into an old house at

Grant's Braes, his mother and sister came to live with him. Agnes remained strikingly beautiful and young-looking with her red hair, red and white complexion, dark eyes and fine forehead. A stone at the roadside marks the site of Grant's Braes, and near to the Gifford Water a well marks the place where Mrs Burns used to fill the family pitcher. It bears the inscription, "Drink of the pure crystals and not only be succoured but refreshed in mind. Agnes Brown, 1732-1820. To the mortal and immortal memory and in noble tribute to her who not only gave a son to Scotland but to the whole world, and whose doctrines he preached to humanity that we might learn".

Towards the end of the Bruntons' time it was becoming obvious that the church would need major repairs. After their departure, Gilbert Burns dealt so successfully with the architects and tradesmen that the new Bolton Church has been described as much a memorial to him as his gravestone in the Bolton Kirkyard where he lies with his three young daughters and his mother and sister. A plaque on the boundary wall outside the church reads:

> *In this churchyard lies the mortal remains of the mother, brother and sister of Scotland's national poet, Robert Burns.*

The Session Minutes for Bolton Church record that on 8 October 1797, Alexander Brunton was admitted minister of the parish on 28 September. At the next Session Meeting it was discovered on examination of the Church accounts that the hearse had brought in £4.19.3d, and the mort cloths 17/4d. Charges for the use of the hearse were, to the poor, 8/- for the first mile with two horses, 10/- if a harness was needed for four horses, plus a shilling more for the keeper each time the hearse went out.

One of the parochial duties which Alexander found most difficult was the need to rebuke members of his congregation who had digressed from the accepted standards of the day. He had to publicly denounce William Bennet and Janet Guthrie for their "irregular marriage". He also had to decide whether the poor should be supplied with meal instead of money, and, at a Parish meeting in April 1803, he had to discover why the poor fund was insufficient. The Church Treasurer's books had not balanced, and £5.16s was owing, but this was remedied and after that the church accounts showed a satisfactory, but small, balance.

The Sunday collection was little more than five or six shillings a month. The Session Clerk was paid £2.2s.0d. out of church funds, and the Bellman was paid £1.1s.0d, for ringing the splendid antique bell in the church tower, inscribed "Michael Burgerhuys me fecit 1618". This is still retained in the present church tower, but two beautiful communion cups, dated 1696, fashioned out of Canongate silver, were sold to aid the maintenance of the church. One is in the Royal Scottish Museum and one in the Huntly House Museum in the Canongate, Edinburgh. Mr Brunton used a much battered pewter dish to anoint the babies of his parish, inscribed, "This is for the Kirk of Boylton 1692".

The remains of an ancient house called "The Orchard", previously the home of John Hepburn, who was executed in 1568 for his complicity in the murder of Lord Darnley at Kirk o'Field, must have recalled to Mary's mind the notorious Gilbert Balfour who conspired in the same event.

Now mistress of her own house, Mary enjoyed the household tasks. Running Cliffdale in a country area among farming tenants had given her an insight into their lives and their problems and helped her to understand the needs of the parishioners in the country around Bolton. She enjoyed the sight of the flocks of women working in the fields wearing the East Lothian "ugly", the bonnet on a high frame designed to protect its owner, and which made even plain girls look pretty. To Mary they looked like bright tropical birds.

The contrast of the gently rolling East Lothian countryside to the flat landscapes and fine seascapes of Orkney encouraged her to draw again. She tried to capture the beauty of the changing seasons in her walks down the lane between the manse and the smithy to the bridge over the river with its overhanging trees. She would cross the field behind the manse and walk beside the stream, absorbing all that she saw. But even in the early days of her marriage, and while still in her early twenties, she was developing the conviction that whatever else she did, she must lead a useful life. Discovering the demands that were made on the minister's time, she supported him in every way possible. She tackled the

Approach to the Bu of Burray

The crest in the outhouse of the Bu of Burray

Mary Brunton

Alexander Brunton

Bolton Manse, Haddington, first home of Mary and Alexander

The Bolton Hearse

Joanna Baillie

D2/8/19

Edinburgh February 5th 1795

My Dear Mrs Craigie

I have the pleasure to inform you that my Aunt has been visibly better these eight days. Her reachings are much less frequent & her spirits much better: while I write she is laying on a sopha singing Its no very lang sin syne — The intense cold of the weather at present is greatly against her; as it precludes all possibility of her going out an airing. — Doctor Wardrop whose very looks must be salutary to the sick, attends her every day & Dr Monro who is the principal physician in the town comes to visit her once a week. — The cold here at present is more intense than any thing I ever felt. I am credibly inform'd that on the night of friday last a thermometer on a level with the snow & with an eastern exposure fell 5 below 0. — My Father is still in London as it is impossible to travel from thence in a carriage. He has had a bad cold but is now quite recover'd. — We expect him down as soon as the roads are passable. — Lady Charlotte Hope has been to see us & I have dined at her house. She is rather pretty, very genteel & has a modesty & sweetness in her manner & appearance which are very taking to a stranger. — We see Mr & Mrs Balfour every day. Their son George is in very bad health. I am much affraid they will lose him. He looks extremely ill & has a bad cough poor thing his mind is weakened with his body & he is much more childish than his sister. — There are a great many little birds sitting on the window picking the crumbs I have laid out for them. I am told there are hundreds found in the fields, frozen or starved to death. — Mr Dewl Monte is just come so I must conclude by desiring my best respects to Mr Craigie & grandmama & subscribing myself my Dear Mrs Craigie

Your Affectionate Niece

M Balfour

First letter of Mary Balfour

economy of the house with imagination, making it as comfortable and elegant as she could, within the strictures of the ministerial budget. One hundred years after Alexander's ministry at Bolton, the minister's stipend did not exceed £157 a year.

Her domestic involvements since leaving school had left her little time for intellectual pursuits. Mr B spent much of his time reading, thinking, preparing sermons and, as a natural progression, discussing with his wife a wide variety of subjects. Her quick intelligence and obvious interest led him to devote more time to leading her into new avenues of reading, and encouraging her into discussion and criticism. His own account of her response to this encouragement gives some idea of her awareness of a need for more knowledge:

> *Her time was now much more at her own command. Her taste for reading returned in all its strength, and received rather a more methodical direction. Some hours of every forenoon were devoted by her to this employment; and, in the evening, I was in the habit of reading to her, books chiefly on criticism and belles lettres. Among other subjects of her attention, the philosophy of the human mind became a favourite study with her; and she read Dr Reid's works with uncommon pleasure. She renewed her acquaintance with our best historians. Her ear was particularly gratified with the music of Dr Robertson's style; and she used often to say that she looked upon his account of the first voyage of Columbus as the most attractive and finished narrative which she had ever perused. She added a little German to her acquisitions in Language. She repeatedly began, but as often relinquished, the study of mathematics. Where the address to the intellect was direct and pure, she was interested and successful. But a single demonstration of the reductio ad absurdam, or by applying one figure to another to show their identity, never failed to estrange her for a long time on that subject. She could never divest herself of an idea that the first had more of the trick of argument than was worthy of pure science; and the second she despised as a mere mechanical operation.*

Dr Thomas Reid and Dr William Robertson, were leaders of

thought in the mid-18th century. Dr Thomas Reid was Professor of Moral Philosophy at the University of Glasgow, and the author of *Inquiry into the Human Mind*; Dr Robertson was Principal of Edinburgh University in 1762, and author of *The History of Scotland during the reigns of Mary and James VI, The History of Charles V*, and *The History of America*. Both had been read and studied by Mr B in his student days. His enthusiasm for their works, and particularly for Dr Reid's philosophy of life, may have formed the early basis for Mary's views on morality which were to be expressed in her novels.

Mr B described her growing interest in literature during their early married life:

> *Her reading was useful to her rather as strengthening her general habits of attention than as leading to marked proficiency in any one branch of study. Her memory, not having been systematically cultivated in early life, was less powerful than her other faculties. She retained the substance of what she read, less by remembering the words of the author than by thinking over the subject herself, with the aid of the new lights which he had opened to her mind. I do not know that, during her residence in East Lothian, she wrote anything beyond an ordinary letter. Even her letters at this period were few. Indeed, her correspondents were always very limited in number. For letter-writing, as either an employment in itself or as a recreation, she had an utter dislike.*

Early in his career, Mr B had been fascinated by the people of the Far East and their language. Keenly interested in the welfare of any young students from that part of the world who were visiting Britain, he invited two East Indians to stay at the manse. Caring for their material needs, and sharing with Mr B in their religious education, Mary found herself examining her own faith more closely. Mr B was pleased:

> *For this important work she had greater facilities now than she had enjoyed at any former period: and she applied herself to it with all her characteristic ardour. Through the grace of God, it gradually led her both to the "knowledge" and to the love of truth*

as it is in Christ ... The Shorter Catechism of our church was the form on which she grounded her instruction to her young pupils; and while, with anxious and successful assiduity, she accompanied its language to their capacity, she never failed to speak in warm admiration of the vigour and condensation of thought by which it is very peculiarly distinguished. Both in her own mind, and in those of her pupils, she was anxious to make religion an active principle, to carry its influence habitually into life. It mingled now with all her pursuits. She sought knowledge, not merely for the sake of the pleasure which it bestowed, but from a strong sense of duty. She loved nature, not for its beauty alone, but for the traces with which it abounds of the wisdom and love of the Creator. Her religion was not a religion of gloom. It shed brightness and peace around her ...

Their marriage was a happy and rewarding one. But the tranquillity of the manse was put to the test when, at the age of thirty, after five years in Bolton, Alexander found himself at that stage of life when a man becomes restless, unsettled, and with an urgent need to test his skills in a wider field. Whatever picture his mother-in-law might have had of him as a penurious country minister, he knew within himself that he now had the experience, and scholastic and theological qualifications, which could qualify him to succeed in a wider field.

Any wife who detects these signs in her husband has the option of turning the blind eye, or offering encouragement. To be confronted with such a dilemma had never entered Mary's mind. She was young enough to "live for the day", happy in her surroundings, happy in her marriage and the widening of her literary horizons, never dreaming that anything would take her into the kind of busy environment which she had always been anxious to avoid.

Mr B also had a dilemma. Convinced that he must improve himself, he also knew how Mary would hate leaving Bolton. So he temporised. In the end, it was Mary who made the move. Women have instincts about these things, and when she understood the situation, she searched for some way to help, and decided to consult her influential godmother, Lady Wentworth. Always willing to pull strings, Lady Wentworth got her husband to write to "Mr Secretary Dundas", Chief Baron of the Exchequer, on behalf of Mr B. The application initially failed, but Mary Wentworth still hoped that Mr Dundas might find something suitable for Mr B. But the post that was eventually offered entailed a decrease in income, so could not be considered.

In the early months of 1801, Mr Dundas resigned, and Mary Wentworth had no way of knowing whether help might still come from him or not. She felt confident that he had had something definite in view for Mr B. But Mr B had little patience with promises from high places, and decided to take matters into his own hands. Edinburgh, where he was born, bred and educated, the focal point of Christianity in Scotland with the historic grandeur of St Giles Cathedral, and the yearly Assembly of the Church of Scotland, was the place where he most wanted to go. He could barely conceal his joy when his application to the New Greyfriars Church in Candlemaker Row was successful. The name of Greyfriars had been prominent in Edinburgh since 1612, when the original church, founded by James I, had taken its name from the monastery built for the monks of Greyfriars. After this church was destroyed in 1718, when some gunpowder stored in the tower by the city authorities exploded accidentally, the new Greyfriars was built to adjoin the west end of the old church.

Alexander's reputation as an attractive preacher, a judicious administrator, and one who was meticulous in the discharge of his parochial duties was in his favour. The fact that he was also a keen Oriental scholar was an interesting extra.

Mary could hardly conceal her dismay. The thought of leaving Bolton, the idea of being irretrievably caught up in the bustle of the capital city – an involvement which she had been so determined to avoid when she refused the invitation to London – filled her with more apprehension than she dared to confess. She experienced the kind of feeling that many young wives suffer when faced with an uprooting from a first home which they have carefully and lovingly cherished. But she loved her husband, and, determined not to stand in the way of his future success, went through all the motions of being delighted.

Mr B was not driven by visions of self-advancement alone.

Seeing how Mary had progressed in the pursuit of literature and Christianity since coming to Bolton, he saw in the move to Edinburgh an opportunity for further development for her. The capital would have more to offer her than he could himself.

Exciting developments were taking place there. The building of George Square, the creation of the office of City Chamberlain, the formation of the Royal Botanical Gardens, the Professorship of Natural History at the University, the opening of the Theatre Royal at the end of the North Bridge on 9 December 1769, and the erection of St Cuthbert's Kirk at the west end of Princes Street had already happened. The creation of the famous Leith Walk and the laying of the foundation stone of the Register House, with full masonic honours, had taken place in 1773. This building, now the Mecca of overseas visitors to Scotland who are tracing their ancestors, owed its existence to a grant of £12,000 from King George III out of money accumulated from the sales of forfeited Jacobite estates. Not until many years later was Alexander Brunton to learn that his wife had a French grandfather who fought for the Hanoverians against the Jacobites, and an Orkney grandfather whose estates were wrenched from him because of his Jacobite loyalties.

Nothing in Scotland had previously been seen to equal the developments that were taking place in Edinburgh at that time. The splendid age of progress appeared in the vigorous spirit that was becoming apparent among the steadily increasing population. Alongside the founding of the Physician's Hall, the Royal Dispensary, the Royal College of Surgeons, the old High School buildings, the penny post and, in 1779, only a few years before the Bruntons' arrival in the city, the earthen Mound, planned to give a second connection between the Old and the New Towns, there was also St Andrew's Church, the Highland Society, the Edinburgh Chamber of Commerce, the New Assembly Rooms founded in George Street in 1778, and the University buildings on the South Bridge, designed by Robert Adam, where the foundation stone was laid to the accompaniment of a great masonic procession.

With stagecoaches speeding up deliveries of mail between Edinburgh, Aberdeen, Glasgow and London, comparing favourably with the 34 hours it had previously taken for a letter to reach Aberdeen from Bolton, and 60 hours for one to reach

London, Mary did her best to view the future objectively, persuading herself of the value of the quicker new mail service between Edinburgh and Orkney. Security measures, even then, had to be tightened up by arming the driver of the coach with a cutlass and pistols.

Firmly dismissing her conviction that the idyllic Bolton life would be forever, Mary cheerfully faced the unwelcome thought of the removal. She unloaded her pent-up feelings in a letter to her mother on 6 October 1802, nearly a year before the departure for Edinburgh:

> *I heartily regret the loss of my little quiet residence, which many nameless circumstances have endeared to me. But when I think that Mr B., without any object in view, might sink into indolence, – live neglected, – and die forgotten, I am in part reconciled to a removal, which will make my wants far more numerous, and my income (all things considered) more scanty. And though I shall never cease to regret Bolton – though I must want many things that I here enjoy; – and what is worst of all, though I can no longer expect Mr B will continue so much to be, as you truly call him, my companion and instructor; I think I could endure anything rather than see him, to please me, consign himself with regret to solitude and inaction. He is pleased with a change that gives him something to hope for (which here he never could have had) and I think I can reconcile myself to anything that gives him pleasure.*

Glad as Mary was to have her mother as a confidante she was also hoping to interest Frances in problems other than her own.

Thomas had died in the early summer of 1799 after a harrowing illness, first diagnosed as pyrexia when he was in Ireland with the Fencibles. When tonic medicines had little effect, he was recommended to try some new steel preparations in London, but these also had little effect. All this was happening at the time of Mary's wedding in the closing months of 1798 when the debilitating illness and the bad weather forced him to stay away, far too weak to stand up to the furore of his wife's anger at their daughter's sudden marriage. Unable to swallow food, he became so weak that he was advised to try the Bath waters. This gave a slight improvement, but there was still the difficulty of eating and drinking – even a glass of the Bath waters gave him nausea. It was a sad decline. Mercury was tried as a last resort but without success. Frances stayed at South Parade, Bath, writing to David Balfour in April 1799, telling him that his brother was neither better nor worse.

Still smarting under the hurt of Mary's marriage, she was determined not to write to her daughter unless specifically asked to do so, and she asked David to forward to Mary a letter from Tom in answer to one she had written to him. The hurt was still so deep that anything the Bruntons did only increased her anger. She told David Balfour:

> *After expressing the most violent anxiety for your brother, they acknowledge a letter I wrote some time ago (one of two I have written since I came here). It lay some days at the Post Office at Haddington where I was desired to direct them, unask'd for. I fancy their anxiety has been so violent to put the means of information entirely out of their heads.*

She asked David to see to Tom's financial affairs which included the sale of the ship he owned called the *Royal Recovery*, and ended her letter by saying:

> *I hope whatever is destined for Mrs Brunton is secured to her and her children.*

From some of the letters which Frances wrote at this time it is obvious that she knew that Tom had a mistress who had given birth to his illegitimate daughter, Charlotte Clifford. Far from being enraged at this discovery, she endured the trauma of seeing her beloved husband battling with a fatal disease, and accepted the child as a part of him, to whom she could transfer her love. Mary never seems to have referred to this child.

Delays in the post made Lady Wentworth's letter of condolence late in arriving after she received Frances's intimation of Tom's death, written on 21 June 1799, so she missed the opportunity of inviting her to stop over with her on her way back north from Bath. Practical as ever, Lady Wentworth now saw herself in the advantageous position of being in close contact with such men of authority as could advance Frances's boys in their careers. Taking it for granted that Tom's eldest son would be accompanying his mother back to Edinburgh after the funeral, she enclosed in her letter of sympathy a letter to the Commander-in-Chief in Edinburgh, recommending her nephew to 'his notice and protection'. She always referred to this nephew as 'Edward' because he had been given that name as a compliment to her first husband. His first name 'John', complimented Tom's wealthy brother who 'was vexed' that he did not arrive in time for Tom's funeral at St James' Church, Bath.

John Balfour felt that he now had the right to monitor his nephew's military career. He interceded with the Commander-in-Chief, Colonel Robert Brownrigg, for John Edward to be restored from half-pay to active service. John Edward was then nineteen. His uncle's idea was for him to join the Expeditionary Force under Sir Ralph Abercromby, the Scotsman who had been a Member of Parliament for Clackmannanshire twenty years earlier. So John Edward Ligonier Balfour joined the English Expeditionary Force under the command of the Duke of York, son of George III, which was defeated by the French armies at Alkmaar in the Netherlands. John Edward, fighting like his grandfather, Francis Ligonier, for the English against the French, was killed, six weeks after attending the funeral of his father.

Mary Wentworth wrote to Frances again:

2 November 1799

I trust time, and your children still remaining will operate in some degree for you as it has done for others in your unfortunate situation . . . Wentworth and I have felt for you most truly and should feel gratified for any opportunity of proving our regard . . . I hope you do not intend in remaining in that melancholy part of the world but tell me in the next to direct to Edinburgh. Have you heard from William, and how does Mrs Brunton go on? William I am particularly interested concerning as I know him best and know he is worthy.

Frances was helpless to push back the waves of desolation and self-pity which engulfed her. She had no near ones at hand any more to help. Mary and Mr B had to try to make her life worth living again. They encouraged her to read to occupy her mind. *Froissart's Chronicle,* Mary said, was "a very large book which entertains me more than anything I ever read before . . . more interesting than most true histories, and more amusing than most fiction". If the price hadn't been so high she would have urged her mother to buy it. Mr B tried to help also. Christian ethics forbade him to bear any grudge against Frances for her strong objections to his marriage with her daughter, and he sent her letters, genuinely concerned that her grief was still affecting her so much after two years:

> *. . . The melancholy which runs through your letter reminds me strongly, if any further proof had been wanting – how dangerous it is both to your spirits and health to winter in Orkney. The return of peace would I trust have ensured your meeting with William who now certainly will have it in his power to leave or at least absent himself from London – with honour – Mary heard from him about a month ago. He was then engaged in the most disagreeable of all duty, the impress service. All his letters speak most warmly in his praise – and I trust that there is reserved for you in his society many a soothing and peaceful day.*

After three years, there were signs that the hatchet might be on its way to being buried between Frances, Mary, and Mr B. When Mr B was experiencing some difficulties with his bank account prior to the move to Edinburgh, Frances got Mary's uncle David, the Writer to the Signed in Edinburgh, to come to the rescue. Mr B was 'deeply affected':

> *Amidst inconveniences which in some shape or other all must feel, I have much to be grateful for. My business with the Bank branch in Haddington is no nearer a settlement than when the embarrassment first arose. I neither deserve nor could have expected the friendly and powerful interest which Mr D. Balfour takes in its arrangement. I can perhaps conjecture by whose suggestion it is quickened.*

Mary, deeply concerned about her mother's continued depression, wrote letters assuring her of her 'warmest affection' and, feeling a sense of personal helplessness in dealing with the situation, turned to the Christian faith for guidance, and told her mother:

> *It is Religion alone that can support the soul. To God's love, my beloved friend, I now commend you. In the hours of separation may he inspire you with comforts which I cannot forsee. In absence may he watch over and protect you. May he unite us again soon, if not in this land of pilgrimage and sorrow, at least in that better country where grief shall intrude no more.*

Life in Edinburgh – The First Novel

Mary approached Edinburgh, buoying herself up with the thought that Mr B would be finding fulfilment there.

Greyfriars was the first church to be built in Edinburgh after the Reformation, and the National Covenant had been signed there in 1638. Mr B, not overawed by preaching in a church with such historic connections, enjoyed its excellent acoustics, and hymns accompanied on the largest organ in Scotland. In the year of his arrival, 1803, he took on the chaplaincy of the volunteer supernumeraries, the Edinburgh Spearmen.

Mary's apprehensions slightly eased when she entered the quietness of St John Street which was to be their home. The houses with spacious rooms, and fine views of the Salisbury Crags, were a connecting link between the Canongate and what is now Holyrood Road. Behind was the garden of Moray House, now built over.

The Bruntons' house was No. 3, at the end nearest to the Canongate, close to the archway bearing the plaque which reads, "The Knights of St John had their houses in this district". Today's premises of the Order of St John in Edinburgh are across the road from where the Bruntons used to live. St John Street, labelled "No Thoroughfare", was a quiet, cheerful locality, guarded by a Street Porter in a faded uniform who barred all entrance to carriages and carts, except those which were for the use of the residents. Almost opposite to No. 3 was the hall of the Canongate Kilwinning Lodge of Freemasons, the oldest Lodge in Edinburgh, and No. 2 of the Grand Lodge of Scotland. Robert Burns was welcomed there.

Once when he attended a meeting of the St Andrew's Lodge at Kilwinning, the Brethren, to his embarrassment, drank the health of "Brother Burns". He described it afterwards:

> *I went to a Mason Lodge yesternight, where the M.W. Grand Master Charteris and all the Grand Lodge of Scotland visited. The meeting was numerous and elegant; all the different Lodges about town were present in all their pomp. The Grand Master, who presided with all solemnity, among other toasts gave "Caledonia and Caledonia's Bard". As I had no idea such a thing would happen I was downright thunderstruck, and, trembling in every nerve, made the best return in my power.*

Sometimes, after these meetings, he would call at No. 13, St John Street, the home of the eccentric James Burnet, Lord Monboddo, lawyer, philosopher, and anthropologist, who explored the possible relationship between men and monkeys, and was credited with the belief that humans were born with tails. But not just to see him did Burns call, nor to sample his magnificent suppers on a table strewn with roses, with bottles of excellent Bordeaux wine similarly garlanded. He was captivated, like many others, by the beauty of Monboddo's youngest daughter Elizabeth. He mentions her in his *Address to Edinburgh.*

> *Dear as the raptur'd thrill of joy*
> *Fair Burnet strikes th'adoring eye.*

But the evenings at No. 13 were never the same after she died from consumption in her early twenties. There were new tenants at No. 13 when the Bruntons arrived. The street, in its quiet seclusion, was a sought-after place of residence for fashionable people. The turnpike stair beside the archway into the Canongate had led to the home of Mrs Telfer, sister of Tobias Smollett, the tall, extremely handsome Scottish-born writer, who had stayed with her when he was writing *Humphrey Clinker.* Mary knew of him from his *History of England from the Revolution to the death of George 2nd,* with its reference to the battle at Lawfield and the heroism of her great-uncle Jean-Louis Ligonier; so her close proximity to the house where he used to stay was exciting. Smollett had found Edinburgh "a hot-bed of genius" where he got to know "many authors of the first distinction" – David Hume, Adam Smith, Hugh Blair, Robert Wallace, Adam Ferguson, and William Robertson D.D..

Sensing, with growing excitement, that Mr B's decision to leave Bolton had not been misplaced, Mary was able to put aside her fears about the dreaded "bustle" of Edinburgh, and begin to settle down.

Before, during, and after the Bruntons' time, St John Street had housed a greater variety of aristocratic, scholastic and commercially-minded residents than any other street in Edinburgh. Alexander Cowan, founder of the paper-making firm at Valleyfield, Penicuik, was at No. 5 – a favourite rendezvous for Sir Walter Scott. The paper for Scott's books probably came from Valleyfield.

Not long before the Bruntons' arrival, Scott had asked his old schoolfriend, James Ballantyne, proprietor of the *Kelso Mail,* to print his first success, *The Minstrelsy of the Scottish Border.* Those who had hardly heard of Kelso were, in Scott's words, "astonished at the example of handsome printing which so obscure a town had produced". After much persuasion, James Ballantyne left the management of the *Kelso Mail* to his brother, and set up his presses at Abbeyhill, near to Holyrood. When Scott was Sheriff-Depute of Selkirkshire he was giving Ballantyne so much legal printing that he had to move to larger premises in the Canongate, and then to even larger premises near the foot of Leith Wynd. Ballantyne chose to live at No. 10, St John Street. There he entertained intimate friends, but when any great event was about to take place in his business, especially on the eve of a new Scott novel, there were, according to Lockhart, "doings of a higher strain in St John Street". Mary never dreamt that Longman, Hurst, Rees & Orme, who published *The Lay of the Last Minstrel,* would be publishing her second novel within 15 years of her arrival in Edinburgh, nor that one of Scott's novels would cause her much heart-searching when she was reading it.

The list of celebrities who lived in St John Street is long. At No. 15 there once lived Dr James Gregory, inventor of the famous

"Gregory's Mixture" which, according to the historian John Comrie, "has been perhaps more universally employed than any other pharmacopial preparation". At a time when doctors were beginning to market mixtures claiming to have remarkable restorative powers, Gregory's Powder, made from rhubarb, ginger and magnesia, was a little gold mine for James.

The Earls of Aboyne, Hopetoun and Wemyss, Sir John Stewart of Allanbank, Colonel Tod, Lady Betty Charteris, the Earl and Countess of Hyndford, and Mrs McLeod, widow of the chieftain of St Kilda, had all lived in the street. Richard Cooper, the line engraver, was an interesting inhabitant. He taught Robert Strange, the Kirkwall-born engraver, who was asked to engrave the plates for the bank-notes which the Jacobites wanted to produce with the design of a rose and a thistle just before Culloden. After Culloden, he was one of the many hunted men taking refuge in Edinburgh where he lodged in St John Street, sometimes sleeping with a long string tied to his toe, the other end hanging out of the window so that his friend could pull on it and have a rope lowered to him when he returned from a drunken spree in the early hours of the morning. In later years, John Thomas Rochead, an architect apprenticed to David Bryce, who masterminded the conversion of Cliffdale to the splendour of Balfour Castle, lived at No. 16.

Frances, after her outbursts over Mary's marriage, found it hard to admit that, after all, she had chosen the right path by marrying Mr B. Bereavement had deprived her of feelings of generosity. When Mr B took Mary and some of his students, including some Indian ones, for a holiday to a house called Springfield near to Queensferry on the shores of the Forth, between May and July 1804, some of the scenery looked so much like Orkney that he thought he'd write a cheerful letter to his mother-in-law:

My Dear Mother – To keep my young Englishmen out of mischief and strengthen my little Indians by sea-bathing, we removed to this place in the middle of May. It answers my expectations in both these respects and adds to these advantages very singular beauty of situation – this you will readily believe when I add that the house stands on a high cliff overhanging the sea – I think the whole aspect is very like an Orkney view. The opposite coast is by no means woody but is marked with beautiful bays and headlands. The sea is studded with little islands and, on a day like this, has all the calmness which even an Orkney calm can boast. Every little sail and every dock is shining in its bright bosom and the smoke of two or three kelp kilns complete the resemblance. We are very retired, and when I have said that we are well, I have exhausted all the news of Springfield growth that can interest you. Mary heard from her brother lately. His Captain I understand is to retire from the service – the eagerness with which his friends have published portions of the evidence which spoke in his favour is considered by the Edinburgh people as a bad symptom of his cause . . . Mary joins me in offering our duty. I am always

Your affectionate and faithful

A. BRUNTON.

Mary soon found a new friend, a Mrs Izett, an untitled Yorkshirewoman, who lived at No. 6. Her husband, Chalmers Izett, had a hatter's business in North Bridge Street. In an environment which still embraced aristocratic and academic neighbours they found simple pleasure in each other's company. Mrs Izett had the Yorkshirewoman's sense of humour and regaled Mary with stories about her neighbour at No. 8, Lord Eskgrove (Sir David Rae), a Lord of Session and Justice Clerk who, in spite of his great ability and strict integrity, had the reputation of being bibulous and eccentric. Once, when passing sentence on a tailor who had stabbed a soldier to death, he tried to impress on the poor man how wrong he had been, saying: "Not only did you murder him, whereby he was bereaved of his life, but you did thrust, or push, or pierce, or project or propel, the lethal weapon through the bellyband of his regimental breeches, which were His Majesty's".

Neighbourliness soon developed into friendship between Mary and Mrs Izett and they enjoyed spending time together, reading and working, exchanging opinions, agreeing and disagreeing, as neighbours do, and discussing literature. This emerged as one of Mary's favourite preoccupations, but she despaired of ever being able to devote sufficient time to it because of her involvements as a minister's wife, and problems connected with her mother and her brother William who, she knew, felt unsettled in the Navy, and under pressure from Lady Wentworth to continue. She was delighted when he married his cousin, Mary Balfour Manson, daughter of their Aunt Elizabeth, who, after her husband's death, gave his house in Kirkwall to William, who used it as his town house while he was living on Shapinsay. It later became the Custom House in Albert Street, Kirkwall.

Frances approved of her new daughter-in-law, and Mary Wentworth wrote to congratulate her:

> *. . . You say so much of your "Belle Fille" that I am apt to applaud my Nephew's choice in preference to a more wealthy bride. The Navy has made him so very cavalierly that I hope Mr Balfour (John) will not regret this step, and it is in his power simply to make recompense for the great disappointment of his lack of promotion in a profession he has followed with much honour and valour altho' not attended with the good fortune he deserved. A happy union I hope will reward his final choice.*

William's first son, Mary's first nephew, and Frances's first grandchild, John, was born on 1 August 1807. Nine months later he died following vaccination in Kirkwall. William received the news at his ship, and, devastated, wrote to his uncle John:

> *I write to prevent you taking any trouble to get me removed to another ship – if you have any interest for good rather use it to get me on shore altogether. I am totally unfit to serve, for what indeed have I any longer to serve for – they have murdered my child – no sooner was my back turned than contrary to my repeated request they took him to Kirkwall and his life is gone – had I been at home he would not have entered that place . . . From the calmness with which his mother writes I am sure he must have been long ill – perhaps he has been little cared for. I expected indeed that he would not meet with the same attention when I was away from home for he always preferred coming to me than any other person. The moment I entered the room he used to stretch out his little hands to me and if anything prevented me*

from taking him he followed me with his eyes until I noticed him and had a thousand ways of showing his satisfaction. What would I not give to recall the last six months? Had I never applied for appointment he might still be living, for knowing that he never kept his health in Kirkwall I never would commit to go there whenever I could avoid it.
. . . If I find that his mother has sacrificed him to her natural indolence I will never while I breathe exchange another word with her . . . What have I left to live for?

Crucifying himself that he had not even seen the little boy before he was buried, his decision to quit the Navy was absolute. Lady Wentworth had to admit defeat and accept that her schemes to get him promoted to the command of the Fleet had failed. She tried to make the best of it by telling Frances that even though the command of a sloop of war would have been desirable, she was sure that William would be happier ashore, and the "belle fille" better off as a poor wife than a rich widow.

After twelve months, William was out of the Navy, back at Cliffdale, his wife forgiven and once more pregnant, and himself now facing a new challenge as factor to Uncle John. Able to face the future with happiness and assurance, he cradled his second son, Thomas, in his arms and felt more ready to steer the fortunes of his family rather than the less human fortunes of a ship of war.

His contentment brought discontent for Frances when she saw her tenure of Cliffdale approaching its end. Lady Wentworth was again ready with advice:

It is very natural that you should quit Cliffdale with regret. After getting over the first unpleasant sensations, I would never inhabit the same house where I had enjoyed happiness and the street would be my pillow in preference to either Cobham or Kirby. I am much for you trying Bath. There you would be secure from dwelling on the past . . .

Frances had mentioned her interest in a child – a little girl, whom she referred to as her "ward". Mary Wentworth wanted to know more, secretly believing that this was Thomas's illegitimate daughter, which it seemed she was. Frances hinted that the little girl lived in Brentwood, and Mary Wentworth was impatient to know more:

> *I can give a good guess who is the father... What name does she go by and what is the woman's name? Where is she? For I have some acquaintance in Brentwood and if I could ever be of any use to her I would, for the sake of the Dear Departed; such a confidence you may be proud of, it was a tribute to your head and heart.*

This "acquaintance" in Brentwood could usefully "enquire a great deal" about the little Charlotte Clifford, making contact with the child by supplying her with books, etc., and so help to satisfy Mary Wentworth's curiosity about her parentage, which was heightened after she learnt that Thomas Balfour had asked to see this child when he was dying.

Mary gives no hint that she was aware of having a sister born out of wedlock to her father, but many of her writings were carefully edited by Mr B after her death, and any such reference he may have considered it tactful to exclude.

Mr B's sphere in Edinburgh widened. He taught the boys at Heriot's Hospital (now George Heriot's School) founded from the fortune of "Jinglin' Geordie", the goldsmith to Queen Anne and King James VI. Robert Southey, the poet, once watched the boys of Heriot's dining off bread and milk, skimming off the cream with their horn spoons.

Elected Honorary Chaplain to the Commissioners of the Northern Lighters, Mr B, in 1807, revised and extended the number of chapters from the Bible which were to be read on board the Lighthouse Tenders and at the Lighthouse Stations. The Lighthouse Board ordered these to be printed along with the Prayer which he composed "for the use of those employed in the erection of the Bell Lighthouse". A Memoranda of the Northern Lighthouse Board states that "this excellent Prayer, with the 'Occasional Prayers', the Doctor afterward accommodated to the Lighthouse Service generally, to assist the Lightkeepers and Mariners at their respective meetings, on the Sabbath Day, for Devotional Exercises".

His main satisfaction lay in seeing Mary settling down and able to mingle with the kind of people whom she had previously admired from a distance:

> *She found herself able to take a share in their conversation; and, though nothing could be further from the turn of her mind than either pedantry or dogmatism, she came by degrees, instead of receiving opinions implicitly, to examine those of others and defend her own. There was a freshness and originality in her way of managing these little friendly controversies – a playfulness in her wit – a richness in her illustrations – and an acuteness in her arguments which made her conversation attractive to the ablest. If they were not convinced by her reasoning, they were gratified by her ingenuity, and by her unpretending openness.*

As Mrs Izett was often busy, and Mary's engagement diary became increasingly full, there were times when she felt the need for a leisure activity. Never one to waste time, she tried to think up a creative pastime which she and Mrs Izett might share and which would form a basis for discussion. One idea was to try writing as a mental exercise, particularly as they were living in the heart of literary Edinburgh after the upsurge in popularity of the work of the young Walter Scott.

Never one to be carried away with romantic ideas of personal success, Mary saw this as just a pastime, a way to experiment with words and phrases just as Grandfather Balfour had done; to think about characterisation and dialogue, the right place for the crisis in the story, and the satisfactory ending. Not just because she was a minister's wife did she incline to the idea that whatever she wrote should have a moral message. Her philosophy of life was that it was necessary to be useful; this, with her conviction of the importance of Christianity to daily living, gave her the problem of setting down what were vital concepts in a way which might bring others to understand them. Usefulness and moral virtue were worthy attributes for the wife of a Church of Scotland minister, but to a large proportion of the general public they were uneasy bedfellows and not the kind of subjects which made for relaxing reading. So this was the initial challenge – how to construct a book with an improving theme sufficiently interesting to appeal to those who were not among the ranks of the pious? Agatha Christie in her novel *The Mystery of the Blue Train* makes her immortal detective, Hercule Poirot, say, "Moral worth is not romantic – it is appreciated by widows". A remark which illustrates Mary's early realisation that if moral worth is to be appreciated it must be clothed in a blanket of romanticism, drama, human weakness, suffering, self-denial and pain.

There was no need to tell Mr B what she was doing, it was just something to fill in odd moments, like sewing or reading. Mr B was needing to co-operate in a ministry that was moderate, and less mistrustful of the State than the presbyterianism of a former generation, a challenge which he was sufficiently broad-minded to accept.

Mary's writing became more absorbing and compulsive, beginning to take on the form of a novel, divided into chapters, with a selection of good and bad characters and a series of events which formed the frame into which she was trying to weave her moral message. It began to flow more easily, and extend her powers of concentration to such an extent that she could hardly put it down. No longer a pastime, it soon got to the stage when it needed a title. *Self-Control* was the one that came to her mind. Tempted to use one that was more alluring, honesty made her discard the thought. The best plan was to call her novel *Self-Control,* and entice any readers who were not put off by the title by writing such compelling early pages that they would have little choice but to read on. So, right at the start, Laura Montreville, the virgin heroine, is assailed, if not quite seduced, by the wealthy rake, Colonel Hargrave, whom she loves:

> *Never had his professions been so ardent: and, softened by sorrow and by absence, never had Laura felt such seducing tenderness as now stole upon her. Unable to speak, and unconscious of her path, she listened with silent rapture to the glowing language of her lover, till his entreaties wrung from her a reluctant confession of her preference.*
>
> *Alight with passion, Hargrave makes Laura increasingly nervous*

and, unaware of his real intentions when he implores her to reward all his 'lingering pains' and 'let this happy hour begin a life of love and rapture', she succumbs.
Pressing her to his breast with all the vehemence of passion, he, in hurried half-articulate whispers, informed her of his real design. No words can express her feelings, when, the veil thus rudely torn from her eyes, she saw her pure, her magnanimous Hargrave – the god of her idolatry, degraded as a sensualist – a seducer. Casting on him a look of mingled horror, dismay, and anguish, she exclaimed, 'Are you so base?' and freeing herself with convulsive struggle from his grasp, sunk without sense or motion to the ground.

Shocked and outraged, she banishes Hargrave for two years, although fully aware that to marry him was the solution to her father's serious money problems. Hargrave's predictable jealousy when she finds a new suitor in Montague de Courcy sparks off an elaborate sequence of events which culminates in her being kidnapped and removed to Canada where she is set afloat in a small boat on a fast-flowing river, alone.

Mr B noticed that Mary was often extremely preoccupied, and was happy that she appeared contented. In the end, it was she who decided to tell him what she was doing. "I cannot help laughing", she wrote, "when I recollect the glowing face and oppressed breathing with which I read the first chapters to my husband; making, in order to please him, a strong effort against my reluctance to the task. Indeed, the book was far advanced before he ever saw it". Mr B reacted well:

A considerable amount of the first volume of Self-Control was written before I knew anything of its existence. When she brought it to me, my pleasure was certainly mingled with surprise. The beauty and correctness of the style – the acuteness of the observation – and the loftiness of the sentiment – were, each of them in its way, beyond what even I was prepared to expect from her. Any encouragement which my approbation could give her (and she valued it for more than it was worth) was received in the fullest measure. From this time forward she tasked herself to write a certain quantity every day. The rule, of course, was often broken: but habit had taught her that a rule was useful. Every evening she read to me what had been written in the course of the day; and when larger portions were completed, she brought the manuscript to me for more accurate examination. I then made, in writing, such remarks as occurred to me and left it to herself to decide upon them. Any little alteration on what had been recently written she was always willing to receive, if she thought it an improvement. But some changes which were suggested to her upon the earlier parts of the story she declined adopting. She had what appeared to me an undue apprehension of the trouble which it might cost her to assimilate the alterations to the remainder of the narrative. But she had little hope, from the first, of the story being very happily combined; and she was only the more unwilling to aggravate, by sudden changes, the harshness of its construction. To its moral usefulness she uniformly paid more regard than to its literary character.

While Mary was working on *Self-Control,* Jane Austen was working on *Sense and Sensibility.* They were close contemporaries; Jane's dates were 1775-1817, Mary's 1778-1818. Each followed the pattern of the young literary-minded ladies of their generation by being enraptured with the works of William Cowper and Walter Scott. But whereas Scott spoke of Jane's writings with a generous display of envy, we find no comments from him on the work of Mary Brunton, a fellow-Scot and near-neighbour to his publisher, Ballantyne.

The vicarage, the parsonage, and the manse, have seen the successful emergence into print of a number of 19th century women – Jane Austen in the vicarage at Steventon, the Brontes at Haworth, Mrs Gaskell as the wife of a Unitarian minister, Joanna Baillie, the daughter of the minister of Shotts, Bothwell and Hamilton, and Mary Brunton, the wife of Mr B. There could be truth in the saying that Calvanistic sermons give a "feel" for language. John Buchan's son, William, believed that his father wrote well because he was a son of the manse and had to sit for three hours every Sunday listening to sermons in his father's church. But this was not where Mary found her inspiration. Mr B, after the enthusiastic greeting for his early sermons on Shapinsay, emerged in later life as a rather uninteresting preacher. The influence of Frances Balfour on her daughter's success as a novelist needs to be considered. Although Frances saw the publication of *Self-Control* two years before she died, no pride in her daughter's achievement appears in her letters to Mary Wentworth. But Frances, who taught French and Italian to her little daughter in Orkney, in the closing years of the 18th century, had made her proficient enough to translate from them fluently and so find the manipulation of language in the compilation of a book less difficult than she had at first imagined.

Literary women in the early years of the 19th century were not universally popular. Aware that they were moving into an area which could be fraught with damaging criticism, their ventures into writing were hesitant and tentative. But their urgent need to break out from the shell of expected domesticity into creativity, encouraged them to be brave.

Self-Control had gone too far for hope of withdrawal. The publishers, Manners and Miller of Edinburgh, had sent it to the printers, George Ramsay & Co., and on 4 October 1810, Mary received the first printed page and was told to expect to receive four sheets a week for the next three or four months. Great news to tell Mrs Izett:

> *October 4 1810*
>
> *I write to-day, not because I am in your debt, for you know you owe me a letter as long as yourself; Ay! Stare if you please – but do not presume to challenge my award – for, know, that I am one of the republic of letters. People are always great upon new dignities; truly mine are new enough. This is the first day of them; this day the first page of fair print was presented to my eyes, and they are to be feasted with 4 sheets a week, for 3 or 4 months to come. You know, dear friend, what is alone necessary to make the feeblest undertakings prosper – Join with me, in begging for all my undertakings that blessing, which in itself is the only true riches, and which bringeth no sorrow with it . . . Ask with me that our Master may make this little work of mine the mean instrument of His glory by promoting virtue, if it be but in one*

heart. Ask for me too, that the sins attending its execution may be pardoned; and that I may be neither elated by its success, nor fretted by its failure. Its failure! the very thought makes my flesh creep! I cannot express to you what a fellow-feeling I now have with the poor wretches whose works fall dead from the press. Well – well – by the end of February, or beginning of March, my rank in the scale of a literary being will be determined by a sentence from which there is no appeal. A hundred things may happen ere then, which will make that sentence of small avail to me, as the forms of clouds that pass over me.

A fair amount still needed to be written when the book went to press but Mary agreed to let the printers start work so that it could be published during the commercially profitable part of the year. Animated by the rush to meet the deadline, she found that what she wrote under pressure was often the best. It was sufficiently professional to be printed from the first copy. Within five days of publication 240 copies were sold. A second edition was called for in just over a month and a third followed, and so *Self-Control* entered the field of best-sellers for 1810.

Like other women authors with a first book, she had it published anonymously. Jane Austen had her *Sense and Sensibility* mentioned in the Morning Chronicle as "A new novel by Lady A-". Mary was extremely apprehensive about the effect of any adverse criticism on the reputation of Mr B were *Self-Control* to be a failure, and her name was on the title page.

After Mr B, Mrs Izett was the first to hear of Mary's reaction to her first taste of fame:

It has come out, the evil spirit knows how, that I'm the author of Self-Control. The report meets us at every turn and is now so strong that our only way is to turn it off without confessing or denying. Of course, all the excellencies of the book are attributed to Mr B, while I am left to answer for its defects. The report has gathered strength from the imprudent zeal of -; who, exasperated by hearing her own sex deprived of any little credit it might have done them, averred, in the heat of her indignation, that "to her certain knowledge Mr B had never written a line of it". The inference was clear - she knew who had. Thus, her authority is added to a report, which, I say again, arose, the evil spirit knows how . . . This is my bad news, and bad enough, though not quite so bad in reality as it was in anticipation. Perhaps it may die away again. If not, there is no help. I must only creep a little closer into my shell; and shrink, if possible, a little more from the public eye.

Now for my good news . . . and first for the best; my highly respected and excellent friend W -, the willing, industrious, and successful disciple of the Master, whose unprofitable servant I am – gives the book his unqualified approbation; and what I value a thousand times more than all the flattering things which have been said, or can be said, of its style and imagery, he says it will be useful. Next, Mr. Miller (the publisher), states the sale to be unexampled here. In five days 240 copies went out of the hands of the publishers. The remainder of the edition is sent to London. How it may do there remains to be seen. Here, it is very much indebted for its success to the attention and friendship of the publishers.

She dedicated *Self-Control* to the Scottish poet and dramatist Joanna Baillie, whose *Plays on the Passions*, was published anonymously in 1806, because she too was aware of the strong bias that existed against women writers. Mary wrote to Miss Baillie to explain the dedication to her:

Madam,

You would smile to hear the insect of a day pay the tribute of its praise to the lasting oak which aided its first feeble soaring – smile then; – for a person whom nature, fortune and inclination alike have marked for obscurity, one whose very name may never reach your ear, offers this tribute to the author of PLAYS ON THE PASSIONS. *The pleasure of expressing heart-felt admiration is not, however, my only motive for inscribing this tale to you. Unknown to the world both as an individual and as an author, I own myself desirous of giving a pledge of spotless intention in my work, by adorning it with the name of one whose writings force every invitiated heart to glow with a warmer love of virtue. On one solitary point I claim equality with you: – In purity of intention I yield not even to* JOANNA BAILLIE.

May I venture to avow another feeling which has prompted this intrusion? What point so small that vanity cannot build on it a resting-place! Will you believe that this trifle claims affinity with Plays on the Passions? – Your portraitures of the progress and of the consequences of passion, – portraitures whose exquisite truth gives them the force of living examples, – are powerful warnings to watch the first risings of the insidious rebel. No guard but one is equal to the task. The regulation of the passions is the province, it is the triumph of RELIGION. In the character of Laura Montreville the religious principle is exhibited as rejecting the bribes of ambition; bestowing fortitude in want and sorrow; as restraining just displeasure; overcoming constitutional timidity; conquering misplaced affection; and triumphing over the fear of death and disgrace.

This little tale was begun at first merely for my own amusement. It is published that I may reconcile my conscience to the time which it has employed, by making it in some degree useful. Let not the term so implied provoke a smile! If my book be read, its uses to the author are obvious. Nor is a work of fiction necessarily unprofitable to the readers. When the vitiated appetite refuses its proper food, the alternative may be administered in a sweetmeat. It may be imprudent to confess the presence of the medicine, lest the sickly palate, thus warned, turn from it in loathing. But I rely in this instance on the word of the philosopher, who avers that 'young ladies never read prefaces'; and I am not without hope, that with you, and with all who form exceptions to this rule, the avowal of a useful purpose may be thought an inducement to tolerate what otherwise might be thought unworthy of regard.

Perhaps in an age whose morality, declining the glorious toils of virtue, is poorly 'content to dwell in decencies for ever', emulation may be repressed by the eminence which the character of Laura claims over the ordinary standard of the times. A virtue which, though essentially Christian, is certainly not very popular in this Christian country, may be stigmatized as romantic; a chilling term of reproach, which has blighted many a fair blossom of goodness ere it ripened into fruit. Perhaps some of my fair countrywomen, finding it difficult to trace in the delineation of

Self-Control any striking feature of their own minds, may pronounce my picture unnatural. It might be enough to reply, that I do not ascribe any of the virtues of Laura to nature and, least of all, the one whose office it is to regulate and control, nature. But if my principal figure want the air, and vivacity of life, the blame lies in the painter, not in the subject. Laura is indebted to fancy for her drapery and attitudes alone. I have had the happiness of witnessing, in real life, a self-command operating with as much force, permanence, and uniformity, as that which is depicted in the following volumes. To you, Madam, I should perhaps further apologise for having left in my model some traces of human imperfection; while, for the generality of my readers, I breathe a fervent wish that these pages may assist in enabling their own hearts to furnish proof that the character of Laura, however unnatural, is yet not unattainable.

I have the honour to be, with great respect, Madam,
Your obedient servant,
The Author.
January 1811.

In time, some of the public began to believe that Joanna Baillie's plays were written by Walter Scott who became her close friend and welcomed her at Abbotsford. He wrote to her in March 1810:

I wish I was like you in everything, but politics in this free country make an early part of our education and become bone of our bone and flesh of our flesh. There is no difference except in words and personal predilections between the candid and well informed of both parties . . .

But while Walter Scott holds his place in Scottish literature, Joanna Baillie has to be rediscovered. In the third canto of *Marmion* he describes her as "the bold enchantress" and compares her to Shakespeare after her *Plays on the Passions* had successful showings in London, Liverpool and Dublin. Her 1810 play, *The Family Legend*, was performed in Edinburgh with a prologue by him. When Lord Byron was dining with his banker in St James's Place,

London, he discussed Walter Scott and Joanna Baillie in the same breath.

Mary felt herself in sympathy with this daughter of the manse – whose "life was sheltered from all harsh contact with the world", and "never shaken by any of the passions that stir the soul of man to the depths". In the early days of Joanna's success, she met a wide selection of literary figures – Wordsworth, Humphrey Davy, Maria Edgeworth, Southey and Coleridge, but developed none of the unpleasant airs which Mary so despised in literary women.

Joanna found Mary's dedication flattering. Her acknowledgment, and suggested alterations to the text were forwarded to Mary by her publishers. Two months after her first letter, Mary wrote to Joanna again:

> *To Miss Joanna Baillie, March 1811.*
> *No circumstances connected with the publication of Self-Control has given me half so much pleasure as your very obliging letter – so kind so natural – so different from some of the pompous strictures, and bombastical praises which have been volunteered on the same occasion! I thank you most sincerely. I should have done so much sooner but that I wished to tell you how far I found it possible to make immediate use of your criticisms. The benefit which I may derive from them in an after work is another consideration. At present I am endeavouring to apply them to the second edition of Self-Control which goes to press next week. I am sorry and half-ashamed, however, to tell you that, though my judgment acquiesces in most of your objections, I have found it impracticable to remove them. The faulty passages are so connected either in truth or in my fancy, with the texture of my story, that I am, or at least, sincerely think myself unable to alter them. Laura, I fear, must continue obstinate; or what would become of the second volume? Pray suffer me to defend another important hinge of my very ill-jointed machine – our Scottish proficiency in painting. The Fourth Edinburgh Exhibition will open in a few days, for the conviction of all sceptics. You have made your censures flattering to me, for I cannot help being pleased when my judgment happens to accord with yours, even though it be somewhat against my book. I have always felt that*

Lady Pelham was a little tedious; I am not at all surprised that you felt it too. Many will feel it who will not have the candour to express their sentiments to me; and few, indeed, would have given that option in terms so gentle – allow me to say, so friendly as yours. I have endeavoured to curtail her ladyship's chidings a little; and would have gone much further upon your suggestion, if I could have found any more passages that could be disjoined. I wish most sincerely it had been in my power to make every correction you suggest.

I have no intention of excusing my faults to you; but if you can have the patience with so much egotism, I can account for them naturally enough. Till I began Self-Control I had never in my life written anything but a letter or a recipe, excepting a few hundreds of vile rhymes, from which I desisted by the time I had gained the wisdom of fifteen years; therefore I was so ignorant of the art on which I was entering, that I formed scarcely any plan for my tale – I merely intended to shew the power of the religious principle in bestowing self-command, and to bear testimony against a maxim as immoral as indelicate, that a reformed rake makes the best husband. For the rest, I was guided by the fancy of the hour. "Me laissant aller doucement, selon la bonne loi naturelle." The incidents were inserted as they happened to occur to my mind, and were joined in the best way I could to those that went before and after.

The thing was not meant at first to see the light; nor would it ever have done so if I had not thought the time it cost me too much to be used in mere unprofitable amusement . . . Anything like praise from you has elevated me to a convenient height above praise or censure.

Mr B is delighted that you approve of the story of poor Jessie Wilson which has always been his favourite part of the book; and I am no less gratified that you praise the American expedition, which is in equal favour with me. Both incidents have shared the fate of the book itself; being reprobated by some, and applauded by others of the literary authorities here. Upon the whole, however, my success has very far exceeded what I ventured to expect. Edinburgh is ready for the second edition long ago, but I have not heard whether we are equally fortunate in London.

Self-Control opens with a five-line quotation from William Cowper's poem *The Task* (Book VI – The Winter Walk at Noon) which Mary thought caught the tone of her book.

His warfare is within. There unfatigue'd
His fervent spirit labours. There he fights
And there obtains fresh triumphs o'er himself,
And never with'ring wreaths, compar'd with which
The laurels that a Caeser reaps are weeds.

She found Cowper, like Robert Burns, satisfying in converting poetry from the earlier scholastic exercise it had been, to the description of the ways of simple men and the beauty of the outside world. But what attracted her most to him was the realisation that his gentle spirit was plagued, as hers was, with doubts about the welfare of the soul.

Mrs Izett, with characteristic enthusiasm, hastened to congratulate Mary on her success, but it was not until 19 April that Mary found time to reply:

I ought to have thanked you an age ago (speaking with feminine hyperbole) for your very kind, very satisfactory letter. Vague praise or censure, even from you, would have brought me neither pleasure nor profit; but, when you descend to particulars you are useful; and in general, agreeable to me. You would be astonished, if you saw how composedly your thin-skinned friend hears both praise and censure. I protest I am often astonished at it myself. If I could believe myself to be so conceited, I might call it a saucy feeling of superiority to the generality of my critics; but it would not be pleasant to think myself so destitute of human humility. Now that you have told me what you think defective in Self-Control, I shall, without reservation, acquaint you with all the faults (as far as I can recollect them) with which it has been charged by others; and shall even candidly confess those which strike myself. To begin with the latter, which, of course, appear to me to have the most foundation; I think the story of Self-Control is defective it is so disjointed – it wants unity. The incidents, particularly in the second volume, have little mutual connection. This appears to me the capital defect of the book. It is patch-work – the shreds are pretty and sometimes rich; but the joining is clumsily visible. You who know how the thing was put together, will easily account for this blemish; but I fear neither you nor I can now excuse or mend it. The American expedition too – though in the author's opinion the best written part of the book, is more conspicuously a patch, than anything else which it contains. Though I do not see the outrageous improbability with which it has been charged, I confess that it does not harmonise with the sober colouring of the rest. We have all heard of a "peacock with a fiery tail"; but my American jaunt is the same monstrous appendage tacked onto a poor little grey linnet. In the middle of the second volume the story lags. An author of more experience would have brought out the characters without such an awful pause in incident. An author of more invention would have contrived incidents to serve that very purpose, as well as to fill up agreeably the necessary time between the close of the first love and the triumph of the second.

The book had 500 pages, three volumes, and 34 chapters. She had told Mrs Izett of its main faults. Other people were all too anxious to find more:

It is alleged, that no virtuous woman would continue to love a man who makes such a debut as Hargrave. All I say is, that I wish all the affections of virtuous persons were so very obedient to reason. As to the faults found with the incidents themselves, "Hargrave bursts upon you too abruptly." "Laura should have been more confidential to Mrs Douglas." "Her proficiency in painting is improbable." "The curricle adventure is trivial." "There is too much Lady Pelham." "The second volume is dull." "Laura should, at all events, have found a means to get rid of Hargrave." "De Courcy's long unsuccessful passion degrades him into a tame despicable being." "The arrest is clumsy, improbable and tedious." "Jessie Wilson is coarse and indelicate." Above all, "The American story is tasteless, extravagent, stale and unprofitable." Nevertheless, the book is read and bought. In spite of all these faults and a hundred more (many of them contradictory) there is not a copy to be had either in Edinburgh or London. I finished the corrections for the second edition last night – and now, what shall I do next? You know I have no great enjoyment in idleness. Meanwhile the hurrying of that vile book into the world has put all my necessary employments far behind. I have letters to write – books to read – presses to put in order – wine to bottle – gowns to make – and all manner of household linen and wearing apparel to mend. Today I have eleven people to dine with me, for which important event I must go and prepare. So it is lucky that my paper is full.

On 30 April, 1811, Jane Austen was writing to her sister Cassandra while correcting the proofs of *Sense and Sensibility:*

We have tried to get Self-Control but in vain . . . I am always half afraid of finding a clever novel too clever – and of finding my own story and my own people all forestalled.

On 11 October 1813, from Feversham, she wrote to Cassandra again:

I am looking over Self-Control again, and my opinion is confirmed of its being an excellently-meant, elegantly-written Work, without anything of Nature or Probability in it. I declare I do not know whether Laura's passage down the American River, is not the most natural, possible everyday thing she does.

By November or December 1814, writing to Anna Lefroy, Jane was expressing her intention of "writing a close imitation of *Self-Control*" as soon as she could:

I will improve upon it, my Heroine shall not merely be wafted down an American river in a boat by herself, she shall cross the Atlantic in the same way, and never stop till she reaches Gravesend.

Not yet buoyed up with the confidence that was to come from

her later writing, Jane was experiencing a twinge of anxiety when comparing her book with the runaway success of this new novel from the pen of the unknown wife of a Church of Scotland minister. But they were never to be rivals, and probably never met. Both were very close in age. Jane had little real reason to suspect that *Self-Control* would overshadow *Sense and Sensibility.* Criticism is made that there are few different types of characters in the novels of Jane Austen or Mary Brunton, the men and women in one story being very like the men and women in another, with only their circumstances changed. But the real skill of these two writers lay in their manipulation of the human content. It is only when Jane skilfully avoids the guilt of open immorality that the gap between them widens. Her religious faith, unlike Mary's open dedication to Christianity, was characteristic of the Anglican reserve. The advent of *Self-Control* with its moral core, gave Jane, the rector's daughter, anxiety. Both these early women novelists, taking exception to any digression from accepted behaviour, encouraged their heroes and heroines, through self-discipline and integrity, to accept and transcend the accepted rules of a society which, however far from ideal, was governed by what was then looked upon as virtue and reason.

In Mary's first attempt at writing she drew on characters and events out of her own experience, and it is not too difficult to detect in Lady Harriet an exaggeration of some of her own mother's characteristics:

> *Her person was shewy, and her manners had the glare, even more than the polish of high life. She had a lively imagination, and some wit…*

Lady Harriet's husband could be a carbon copy of Thomas Balfour:

> *Captain Montreville was of a family ancient and respectable, but so far from affluent, that, at the death of his father, he found his wealth, as a younger son, to consist only of £500, besides the emoluments arising from a lieutenancy in a regiment of foot. Nature had given him a fine person and a pleasing address; and*

H

to the national opinions of a Scotish (sic) mother, he was indebted for an education, of which the liberality suited better with his birth than with his fortunes. He was in London negotiating for the purchase of a company, when he accidentally met Lady Harriet . . .

This gives us a clue to the meeting of Thomas and Frances, and the following excerpt sketches out what the circumstances may have been in reality:

As his regiment was at this time under orders for the West Indies, Lady Harriet prevailed on him to exchange to half-pay; and her fortune being no more than £5,000 economy, no less than the fondness for solitude natural in young men in love, induced him to retire to the country with his bride, who had reasons of her own for wishing to quit London. He had been educated in Scotland and he remembered its wild scenery with the enthusiasm of a man of taste . . . to relieve his conscience from the load of utter idleness at twenty-three (he) began the superintendence of a little farm. Here the ease and vivacity of Lady Harriet made her for a while the delight of her new acquaintance. She understood all the arts of courtesy; and, happy herself, was for a while content to practise them.

The expression "for a while", twice repeated in the extract, emphasises Frances's ephemeral success in Orkney. There are other indications that she and Lady Harriet are similar, if not identical:

Lady Harriet's spirits had ebbs – her days passed in secret discontent or open murmurings – Montreville . . . was on the point of returning to his profession, or of seeking relief in such dissipation as he had means of obtaining, when the birth of a daughter gave a new turn to all his hopes and wishes.

The first chapter of *Self-Control* is autobiographical. Mrs Douglas, the wife of the parish clergyman is probably Mary Craigie, "reserved in her manner, gentle in her temper, pious, humble and upright . . . beloved without effort to engage the love, respected without care to secure the praise of man". She was the person to whom Laura (substitute Mary) could go for help and advice and the initiation into the Christian faith which Lady Harriet had been educated to despise.

With her fairly limited experience of the world, Mary drew on known people and personal happenings. Laura's love for Colonel Hargrave began when she was seventeen – the same time in life when Mary's had begun for Mr B. The description of the village churchyard at "Glenalbert" could be Bolton:

> *The church itself stood detached from the village, on a little knoll, on the west side of which the burial-ground sloped towards the woody bank that bounded a brawling mountain stream . . .*

Laura's departure to London with her father, visiting Edinburgh en route, led Mary to describe her own feelings when Laura, after admiring the Castle rock and the features of the Old Town, took a walk, "not without some dread of encountering the crowd which she had expected to find in such a city":

> *At this season of the year, however, when Laura reached Edinburgh, she had little cause for apprehension. The noble streets through which she passed had the appearance of being depopulated by pestilence. The houses were uninhabited, the window-shutters closed, and the grass grew from the crevices in the pavement . . . As they passed the magnificent shops, the windows gay with every variety of colour, constantly attracted Laura's inexperienced eye . . . The next thing which drew Laura's attention was a stay-maker's sign. "Do the gentlemen wear corsets?" said she to Montreville. "What makes you inquire?" "Because there is a man opposite who makes corsets. It cannot surely be for women."*

Edinburgh etiquette in the early 19th century taught Laura (and possibly Mary) that a certain time must elapse between a fashionable invitation and the subsequent visit. Laura is at a loss to understand why a lady could really be engaged for four daily meals on two succeeding days. She and her father fill in their time by visiting the castle and the public libraries, and Laura sees what can only be Mary's beloved St. Leonard's:

> *... Nothing in its singular environs more charmed the eye of Laura than one deserted walk, where, though the noise of multitudes stole softened on the ear, scarcely a trace of human existence was visible, except the ruin of a little chapel which peeped fancifully from the ledge of a rock...*

Laura and her father made the journey to London by sea, taking six days, a cheaper form of travel than by coach, and possibly one that Lieutenant Thomas Balfour took when going south to join his regiment.

If Mary had based the characters of Montreville and Lady Harriet on her parents, Montague de Courcy may have been based on her brother William. Some of Frances's qualities may also have come out in Lady Pelham. *Self-Control* was published two years before Frances's death in 1813. Whether she ever read the description of Laura's proficiency at the piano and her fluency in French and Italian, and linked it with the days in Orkney when she was teaching these skills to Mary, will never be known.

Concentration on the book for long periods affected Mary's health. Mr B summed up the situation by saying that her condition "made it desirable that we should visit Harrogate", so they set off with the Izetts in the autumn of 1809. Mary's wrote to her mother from there:

> *We drove through a country flat as the floor, to a little village called Wigton; and from thence to Keswick by a tremendous road; but leading at last through the Vale of Bassenthwaite, one of the sweetest of all prairies riantes. The day which we spent in Keswick was the finest possible – not a breath of wind, and scarcely a cloud in the sky. We waited and wandered about till it was quite dark. Great was my desire to take up our rest there for a fortnight, for in "the Grange", the sweet little hamlet at the mouth of Borodale, there was a parlour and bed-chamber to be let furnished! Dread Lowdore is the most picturesque waterfall I*

ever saw; but no more to be compared with Moness in magnificence, than a little coquette, tricked out in gauze and gumflowers, with the simple majesty of Milton's Eve . . . The Lakes are truly lovely, though not quite so unparalleled as when I last saw them; for I have since seen Loch Lomond; nor do I think they can be compared in sublimity with the approach to Loch Katrine. Did you ever see Kirby Lonsdale? It is the most rural, pretty interesting place imaginable. It is a true English village – English in its neatness – English in the handsomness of its houses, (Scotch handsome houses are seldom built in villages) – and English, above all, in its church-yard – smooth as velvet – green as emeralds – clean, even to the exclusion of fallen leaf from one of the tall trees that surround it! From this church-yard, situate on a high bank overhanging the river Loan, you command a fine view of Lonsdale, rising here and there into gentle swells – gay with woods and villas. The river is not very English; for it is a rapid, lively, transparent stream not creeping sluggishly through rich meadows, but dancing gaily to the sun, or dashing against tiny rocks into Lilliputian waves . . . Nous voila at Harrogate! and I believe there is no place in Britain to which you would not sooner accompany me. One hundred and forty people dine with us daily – all dressed as fine as Punch's wife in the puppet show. Do but imagine the noise of so many tongues – the bouncing, banging and driving of eighty waiting-men – the smell of meat sufficient, and more than sufficient, for one hundred and forty cormorants – and all this in the dog days!!! Harrogate itself is a straggling village, built on an ugly sandy common, surrounded with stunted black Scotch firs – the only thing in shape of tree or shrub that never can be an ornament to any possible place. From a hill above Harrogate there is a view of prodigious extent over the richest and largest plain which I have ever seen. York, which is twenty-two miles distant, seems nearer than the middle of the landscape. Mrs I (Izett), who is an Englishwoman, was in ecstacies. For my part, I must confess that I think a little rising ground, or even a mountain, no bad feature in a landscape. A scene without a hill seems to me about as interesting as a face without a nose!

****

Here is Mrs - an elderly Scotchwoman, with a great memory and a little understanding, who has read her head full of facts – fuller than it can hold, for they are always bursting out – but who has not wit enough to draw any new conclusion from them. She is always talking of "talent"! The word gives me a qualm. Then there is –, whose bright eyes look into everything, but not through it. He talks incessantly and almost amusingly. He has made a capital mistake in his choice of a profession. He ejaculates about a picture with much more energy than he says grace. He loves a good dinner, and hates John Knox. There is -. She is a little repulsive in her first abord. Most plain people are so, especially if they have pretty sisters; they are not accustomed to expect to please. She looks good-humoured, however, when she smiles; and talks warmly of home, and kindly of her sisters. She speaks shortly and abruptly, but not ungenteely, and she never mentions "talent" or "liberality". Next there is a certain – a quiet sort of man, with more in him than one would think – with some wit, some fun, and a good deal of commonsense – but enough of humour made up of pride, modesty, and laziness to keep him commonly in the background. However, it passes pretty well; for people applaud their own penetration if they find him out; and that inclines to give him credit for more than they can discover. His little fat wife is a good-humoured wholesome-looking creature – not very captivating to strangers certainly, yet I cannot exactly tell why. It is said she has a good understanding, and I believe it; but the elephant is so slow in his motions that the veriest hack – nay, an actual ass makes a better figure in the common jog-trot way. As to character, she is certainly an original – but with so many littlenesses, inconsistencies, and offities, that the picture would take more time than it is worth.

Another holiday letter went to Aunt Craigie, early in 1810:

Studley Royal is truly a noble place. Besides a park of 1,100 acres, adorned with timber of unequalled magnificence, there are 300 acres of pleasure-ground kept with a neatness of which I had no previous idea. The lawns are as smooth and as equal in colour and texture as green velvet; and though they, as well as the gravel-walks, are shaded by lofty trees, and embellished with an endless variety of flowering shrubs, not a fallen leaf – not a twig is suffered to derange their neatness. The place is laid out in the old-fashioned style, with circular pieces of water, statues, temples, cascades flowing over flights of steps, and banks made by rule and plummet. Nevertheless, the place is not only beautiful, but magnificent; the ground is naturally swelling and varied; the artificial river is so large, that you forget it is the work of man; the temples, though a little out of place, are still beautiful and the smooth shaven lawns show to great advantage the dark majesty of the woods that tower over them sometimes to the height of 120 feet. But above all, Studley contains one charm which, so far as I know, is altogether matchless – the ruins of Fountains Abbey. This noble pile – but how can I describe it to you? No words that I can use will give any idea of its beauty, or of the effect which it had on me! Sometimes the very recollection of it fills my eyes with tears. I can convey some notion of the magnitude of the building by telling you that it still covers two acres of ground, and that it once extended over ten; but to describe the effect of the whole is out of my power. Imagine the huge folding doors thrown open to usher you into a cathedral of prodigious extent. The roof is gone, the noble pillars, of more than Corinthian lightness, which once supported it, still spread here and there into broken arches, twisted with ivy; which clothes, but does not conceal their forms. Large trees, rising from the dismantled court, mingle their giant arms with the towers. – The windows – but why should I attempt an impossibility! I protest I will never again try to give an idea of Fountains Abbey! To crown it all, I had scarcely heard the place mentioned, and never had read an account of it; so that it burst upon me at once in all its glory.

My companion, who is an Englishwoman, maintained a long dispute with me on the comparative merits of Studley and Dunkeld; she, of course, preferring the beauties of her own country, and I, as in duty bound, upholding the honour of mine. The woods of Dunkeld are almost equal in magnificence. The river is superior; as all the works of its mighty Maker are to those of man.

The mountains of Dunkeld are incomparable, but I confess that Scotland has no Fountains Abbey.

After returning home Mary wrote to Aunt Craigie again:

According to the different styles which prevailed at the different times when York Minster was rearing, it exhibits every variety of Gothic architecture. The whole, notwithstanding its sublime extent, has an air of astonishing lightness and grace . . . I could not help smiling at the insignificence to which the human form was reduced, as we stood, compared with the gigantic features of the building. Stone saints, as large as Mr B, furnished Lilliputian ornaments for some of the screens. We were so fortunate as to be there at the hour of evening prayer, and heard the evening service chanted. If I might say with reverence that any earthly worship was suitable to its object, I should say that the service at York was not worthy of him, in so far as man could make it so, except in one point. In this vast temple, echoing to music which might well be called heavenly, none but the hirelings came to worship; excepting the paid singers, there were not six persons present. To this structure belong priests of all ranks – clerks, singing-men and singing-boys. A superb establishment is kept up. Nothing is wanting to the service, except that what the Lord of hosts prefers to every temple – humble and devout hearts. I staid there nearly two hours, and came away long before I was satisfied with gazing. As for poor Mr B, he is gone York-Minster mad.
The next day's journey lay through a pretty smiling country; with much more appearance, and much less reality of richness than East Lothian. This apparent richness is caused by the innumerable hedgerows. I verily think there is not a field of twenty acres in the whole "North Riding". I saw hundreds of the size of your garden, inclosed with double hedges. These are a great ornament to the country. Indeed, it is so flat that it could be quite ugly without them. But the ground cannot be very productive where the owners waste so much of it on fences. In the richest part of East Lothian, not a hedge is to be seen. There is not much corn in Yorkshire, and still less grass. It is a grazing country; meadow-grass seems the chief object of the farmer. By the bye,

its verdure is infinitely finer than that of sown grass, and this is another cause of the smiling air of the fields.

On entering Durham every thing changes. The country becomes bare and hilly – a doleful strife between English dullness and Scottish sterility! – Every coal country that I ever saw is dreary; as if it were intended that comfort should be cheap within doors, where there is nothing to invite one abroad.

As you approach the Border, the Scotch farming begins to prevail. Large fields of turnip and clover – few hedges – trees only planted in clumps where little else will grow. The country on the English side is far from being pretty. Indeed, by whatever road you enter Scotland, it gains by comparison for the first stage. We crossed the Tweed by a beautiful bridge at Coldstream; and, to confess, my heart leapt lightly as I drew in the breath of my native land. We Scots folk shook hands heartily, and declared that we had seen no such river in England; nor any vale like that in which its waters were glancing bright to the sun. – turned a mournful eye towards her own country; but at Kelso, where first we alighted, even she confessed that no English town could boast a finer situation. It stands at the junction of the Tweed and the Teviot. Both are fine streams, and flow here through a lovely country, rising into sunny slopes, or shelving into woody dells, or sinking into rich meadow. The Eildon hills tower at a distance, and are highly ornamental to every scene of which they form a feature.

. .

The road to Edinburgh lies through the Lammermuir range of hills. For miles, little but heath meets your eye. At last, without any warning, on reaching the ridge of Soutra, all the rich Lothians burst on your sight, spread like a map at your feet! Edinburgh towers with its rocks in the middle, and the majestic Forth widens slowly into a sea. I have often gazed at this prospect, yet still it strikes me as the most magnificent which I have seen. It is unrivalled in extent, richness and variety; and though I think closer scenes are more interesting, this, I am persuaded, no one can look on without pleasure.

But no pleasure which mere beauty can give, ever equalled that which I felt at this first distant glimpse of my home – my home, to which, wherever I travel I always return as to the arms of a friend! Have we not reason to bless the goodness which has so ordained that many a home, possessing no other charm, yet charms us because it is our home? But mine has many, many comforts. If I could share them with you, and two or three other persons dear to me, it would want none to make it complete to me. This cannot be! But I trust we shall meet in a home which will, indeed, be complete to us all, and who knows whether our propensity to love the place with which we are familiar may not be one of the means of endearing us to that better home throughout eternal ages.

Widening horizons helped Mary to gain in confidence, and her cheerfulness, modesty, generosity and compassion soon brought her popularity. Born at a time when the bloodthirsty nations of the world were becoming more orderly, she practised her faith in such a way as to avoid any showy evangelism, keeping private the personal Christianity which led her to compile her *Helps to Devotion,* carefully selected from the Bible.

After the holiday, Mr B heard that he had succeeded in his application to become one of the ministers at the Tron Parish Church in Edinburgh. Situated at the corner of the High Street and the North Bridge, it was another of Edinburgh's historic churches, founded in 1637, and taking its name from the nearby public weighing-beam, the tron. During Mr B's time as minister there a great fire broke out in Assembly Close and set the steeple ablaze. It was the most disastrous fire in the city's history, and destroyed all the buildings on the south side of the High Street from the head of the Old Assembly Close to the Exchequer Buildings in Parliament Square. The Tron steeple blazed furiously, and firemen had to fly for their lives when the molten lead poured down. The steeple crashed, but the church was saved. After threats of demolition, and after being closed for thirty-five years, its doors were officially opened in June 1987, by the Moderator of the General Assembly, the Right Reverend Duncan Shaw.

Mary's happiness at Mr B's appointment was followed by dismay when she learnt that the Izetts were moving from Edinburgh to Kinnaird, near Dundee. But they continued to exchange letters. Mary wrote her first in the spring of 1810:

. . . You are now sixty miles distant from Edinburgh, and I have lost what probably no time will restore to me, that "medicine of life" which is promised that they shall find who have received a title to higher rewards. Since you left me I have a hundred times determined to write. I need not assure you that forgetfulness has had no share in my silence. Levity itself would not forget a friend (if levity could have a friend) in one month – "one little month!" I am reminded of you by all my business and all my pleasures; for – which of my pleasures did you not heighten and in what branch of duty did you not stimulate me? But all that is over! and I can only repent that I did not better use what might have been so eminently useful. I thank you heartily for your account of your rambles at Kinnaird – would that I were the companion of them! In return, you shall learn my methodical routine. I write part of every forenoon, and walk for an hour or two before dinner. I lounge over the fire with a book, or I sew and chat, all the evening. Your friend Laura proceeds with a slow but regular pace, a short step every day – no more! She has advanced sixty paces, alias pages, since you left her. She is at present very comfortably situate, if the foolish thing had the sense to think so; she is on a visit to Norwood, where she is to remain for a few days; and a very snug old-fashioned place it is! Though it should never be laid open to the public at large, you shall see the interior of it one day or another.

The Izetts' departure from Edinburgh to Kinnaird set the Bruntons thinking about a country escape for themselves and decided on one at St Leonard's at the entrance to the Queen's Park in Edinburgh, once mentioned by Walter Scott as "a sequestered dell". Mary told Mrs Izett:

Last Thursday I paid a visit to our chateau in St Leonard's; though nothing has as yet the least tinge of green, it did not look very ill. It is as gay as ten thousand purple crocusses, and twice as many yellow ones can make it. I shall soon grow impatient to take possession and, if we manage it, I believe we shall revert to our plan of going there early, if not, I must just console myself with my friend Laura in Edinburgh. I wish I saw the end of her; but

> *"wilds immeasureably spread seem lengthening as I go". If I ever undertake another lady, I will manage her in a very different manner. Laura is so decently kerchiefed, like our grandmothers, that to dress her is a work of time and pains. Her younger sister, if she ever have one, shall wear loose, floating, easy robes, that will slip on in a minute . . . We old folks make friends slowly – so slowly, that I believe life will be too short to furnish me with another such as you; therefore I value you accordingly. I hope that we shall be neighbours in another world, or, that if your place be, as it well may, a higher one than mine, you will not be forbidden to visit the meaner mansions of our Father's house.*
> *I am going to visit the person that has come to No. 6. I believe I shall hate her; yet they say that she is pleasant. If she sits in the same place where you used to work, I think I shall beat her. They say that narrow-minded people always hate their successors. I must be the most illiberal of all creatures, for I hate the successors of my friends.*

As she was spending so much time writing, Mary wondered if she could encourage Mr B to write also. Once, when they had a publisher friend to dinner, she asked if he would consider being her husband's publisher and was surprised to hear him say that he would just as soon publish something of hers. She passed this off as just a socially polite remark, but rather a surprising one if he had not heard that she was writing. All that Mr B had published was connected with his work. His *Outlines of Persian Grammar, with Extracts* became a recognised textbook (1822). He also compiled *Extracts from the books of the Old Testament, with Sketches of Hebrew and Chaldee Grammar* (1814) and *Outlines of a speech intended to have been delivered at the General Assembly* (1815). In 1848 he published *Forms for Public Worship in the Church of Scotland.*

This throw-away remark by their dinner guest took root in Mary's mind and she felt it a challenge to bring her book to publication point. Mr B was enthusiastic, Mrs Izett was supportive, and now that the novel was developing well, Mary felt that she might produce a work which might bring the kind of reaction from the public for which she hoped. In the summer of 1810 she wrote to Mrs Izett again:

Madam

I am favor'd with your Ladyships Letter of the 15th, by this Post, and do not lose a moment in assuring you, that I will take an early opportunity to employ Dr. Balfour, having the honor to be with great respect

Your Ladyships
Most obedient
Humble Servant
St. Vincent

Rochetts
30th July 1802

Lord St Vincent's letter to Lady Wentworth

Tron Church

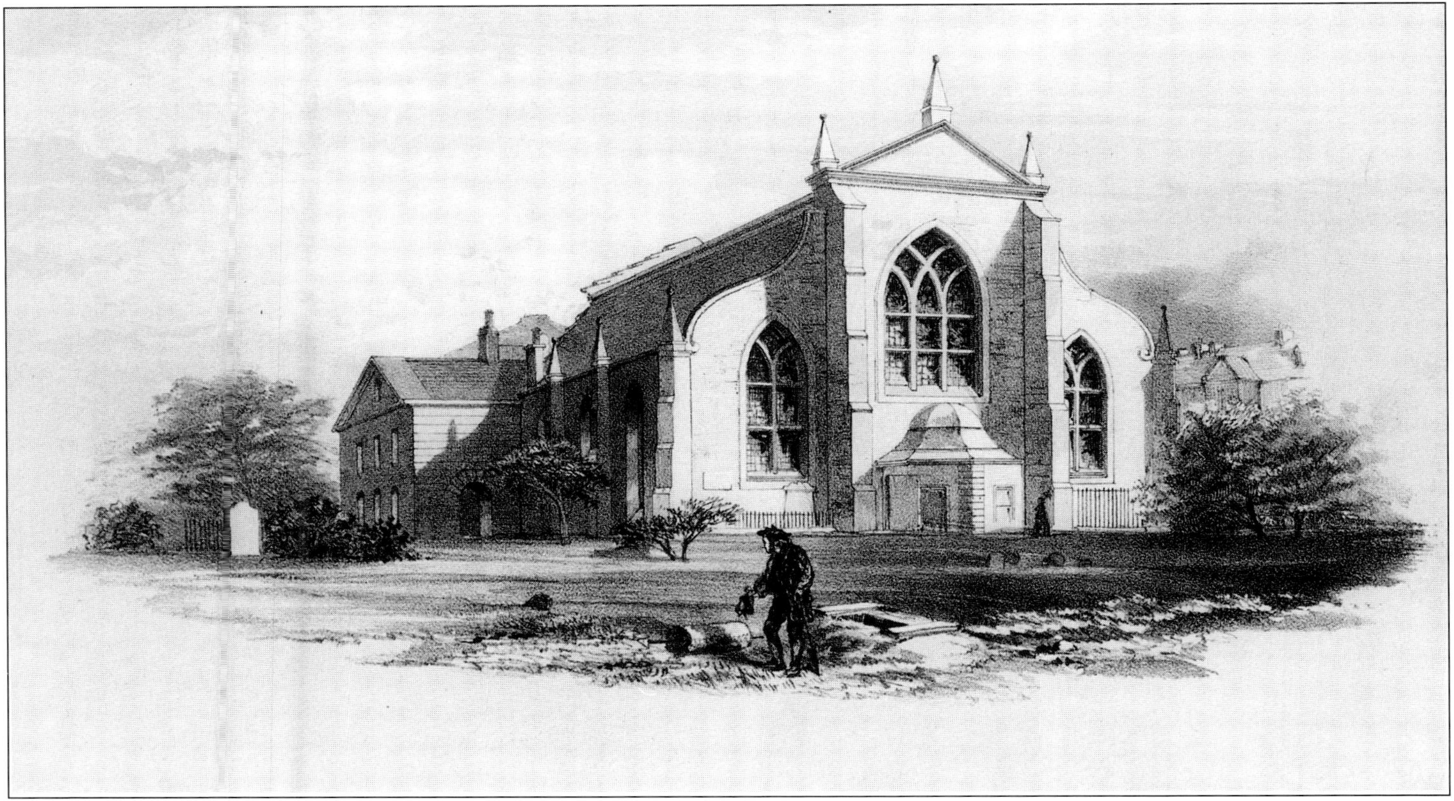

Greyfriars Church

Kilwinning Lodge, St John Street, where Burns was a guest – opposite the Brunton's house

35, Albany Street

The Warwick Vase in the Burrell Collection, Glasgow

Distraining for Rent

James Watt's workroom

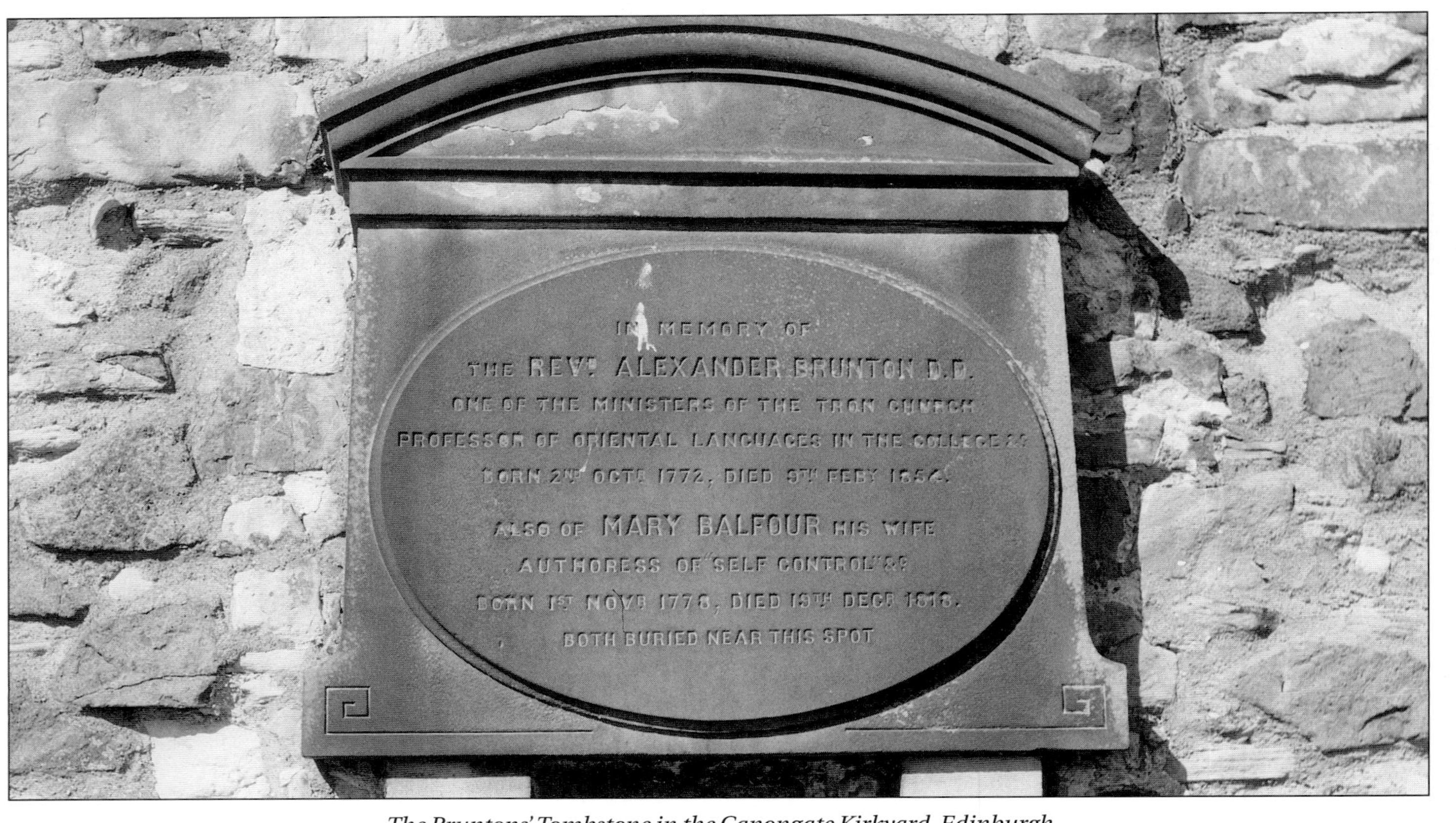

IN MEMORY OF
THE REVD ALEXANDER BRUNTON D.D.
ONE OF THE MINISTERS OF THE TRON CHURCH
PROFESSOR OF ORIENTAL LANGUAGES IN THE COLLEGE
BORN 2ND OCTR 1772, DIED 9TH FEBY 1854.
ALSO OF MARY BALFOUR HIS WIFE
AUTHORESS OF "SELF CONTROL" &c
BORN 1ST NOVR 1778, DIED 19TH DECR 1818.
BOTH BURIED NEAR THIS SPOT

The Bruntons' Tombstone in the Canongate Kirkyard, Edinburgh

If I haven't answered your letter, blame not me . . . nor Mr B, who has teased me every day to write to you. Blame your dear friend and favourite, Montague de Courcy, Norwood, Esq., he has been making love so energetically that I had not the heart to leave him in the middle of his flames . . . I have been far more compassionate towards him than she who ought to have been the most deeply interested. She has not only given him his conge, but has barbarously left him, in a cold October evening, standing under a tree in his own venue. There he has stood since last night; there he must stand all today, for today I write to you; all tomorrow, for I go to town; and all Thursday, for I do not return till then . . . I must take more exercise if I would not be sick, and must sew more if I would not be ragged . . .

The idea of publication was approaching reality. Panic at the thought of it convinced Mary that the book would be a failure. She couldn't think of publishing it under her own name for fear of adverse repercussions on Mr B. Praise mattered little to her – severe criticism was another matter, seeing that her husband was now such a well-known figure. The idea of becoming famous, were that ever to happen, appalled her. In her confusion and uncertainty about the future of *Self-Control* she had to write to Mrs Izett again:

My hopes of popular favour are low – very low indeed. Of a work like mine, the wise and the good will not be at trouble to judge. Its faults are not such as will recommend it to the vulgar. It may become popular, for that is a mere lottery. If it do so, dear friend, its faults, of which it has many, will draw down the censure of those who are, or think themselves entitled to decide for their neighbours. Now, will not one bitter sarcasm on it, much more on its author, give you more vexation than the praise of nine-tenths of novel readers will give you pleasure? I judge by myself; for while I have little pleasure in praise, I am on many subjects keenly alive to censure. Many a person less generally vain than I, has felt all the touchy vanity of authorship. But I am positive that no part, no, not the smallest part – of my happiness can ever arise from the popularity of my book, further than as I think it may be useful. I would rather, as you well know, glide through the world unknown, than have (I will not call it enjoy) fame, however brilliant. To be pointed at – to be noticed and commented upon – to be suspected of literary airs, to be shunned, as literary women are, by the more pretending of the other! My dear! I would sooner exhibit as a rope-dancer. I would a great deal rather take up my abode by that lone loch on the hill, to which Mr. I. carried my husband on the day when the mosquitoes were victorious against him.

The First English Holiday and the Second Novel

The year following the publication of *Self-Control*, saw Mr B's application for the Professorship of Hebrew and Oriental Studies at Edinburgh University. Born in Edinburgh, educated there, and with over six years' experience as a minister in its churches, he felt that the appointment could be within his reach. For his referees he chose William Ritchie, co-founder of *The Scotsman* newspaper, and Rev. Hugh Meiklejohn.

Mr Ritchie wrote:

Mr Brunton has been extending his inquiries beyond the classics of Rome and Greece, and has, for a great number of years, been devoting a large portion of his time to the study of Hebrew, of Persic, and of such kindred tongues as are conducive to the just interpretation, and critical analysis of our ancient scriptures. He has thus, without the shadow of ostentation, in the effort for self-improvement in the line of his profession, been prosecuting exactly that kind of study which qualifies him for filling a Hebrew chair. Those who know anything of Mr Brunton and his studious habits, will not call in question the high proficiency which, in such a number of years he must have made. And therefore, from his acquaintance with the appropriate languages; from the high respectability of the character which he maintains as a minister; from his distinguished talents for chaste and elegant composition, and his happy facility for the communication of knowledge, with simplicity and perspicuity; from the virtues of his private life, and his amiable manners; from all these, I feel myself not only warranted, but bound, from intimate conviction, and the clear persuasion of my mind to declare, that I think Mr Brunton eminently qualified to fill the chair of Professor of Hebrew in such a manner as to reflect honour upon himself, to promote the diffusion of Biblical literature among the students of divinity, and to maintain, in his sphere, that high rank in the literary world which our University has attained.

Rev. Meiklejohn, closely associated with the Department of Hebrew, and having known Mr Brunton as a Divinity student, believed that he would be helpful to the students of Hebrew Literature, and a credit to the University. Before writing his testimonial, he studied Rev. Brunton's letter to the Provost of 15 June 1812, which read:

My Lord – May I request to offer myself to the notice of your Lordship and the Town Council as a candidate for the office of Professor of Hebrew in the University of Edinburgh. I entreat your Lordship to be assured that I would not presume to take this step without being conscious of possessing, in some degree, the qualifications necessary for discharging the duties of the situation at which I aspire, or without feeling the strongest wish to merit by every exertion in my power, the patronage which I thus venture to solicit. I have the honour to be, with the greatest respect, My Lord, Your Lordship's most obedient and faithful humble servant,

ALEXANDER BRUNTON.

Three weeks later, Rev. Meiklejohn wrote to the Lord Provost:

. . . I cannot be supposed indifferent to the manner in which the Theological Chair in our University, now vacant, is supplied. The study of Hebrew is most intimately connected with the department which I have occupied for a very considerable number of years; and I feel most anxious, that the Professor appointed should be creditable to our University, and useful to the students of Theology. This has become of still greater importance, from the tendency which has appeared, during the last years, to prosecute Hebrew Literature with an ardour formerly

unknown in this country. Having the honour to be in some degree known to your Lordship, I shall be forgiven for writing this letter, more especially as it is done under the conviction that you will be disposed to listen to any information respecting the different candidates suggested to your notice.

Mr Brunton, one of the Ministers in your City, has been known to me since the period when he himself was a student in Divinity, and with a greater degree of intimacy than almost any other members of the church. I have been acquainted with the nature and progress of his literary pursuits, and which have been of a description which the public could not hitherto know or appreciate. It is now more than seven years since his labours were zealously devoted to the language of the Old Testament, and the result has been a knowledge of it equalled by few and surpassed by none of our Scripture Critics. To other Oriental tongues, his attention has also been directed; and though here I am not personally inclined to judge, I am persuaded that his attainments will be found to be respectable. Knowledge in the department is most unquestionably and indispensably necessary; but there are other points of character which deserve the most serious consideration. One of these is unwearied perseverance and fidelity in the discharge of professional duty; and in this respect, Mr Brunton has given a pledge to the public, which must be held most completely satisfactory. There is, therefore, in his case, the most perfect security against disappointment. I am very little disposed to obtrude my opinions in matters of this kind; but I have the satisfaction of knowing that they are in unison with those entertained by others actively employed in the instruction of that class of students to whose improvement the labours of our Hebrew Professor must be devoted. We are fully convinced, without regarding personal attachments and aversions, and on a firm estimate of Mr Brunton as a man and a scholar, that his appointment would be creditable to the university; highly beneficial to our students in theology; and do honour to those who have the power of making it. I have the honour to be, with the greatest and most sincere respect, My Lord,

Your very faithful and most humble servant,

HUGH MEIKLEJOHN.

But the impressive rhetoric did not initially secure the Chair for Mr B. It went to Dr Alexander Murray, minister of Urr in Kirkcudbrightshire, the largely self-educated shepherd's son from Dunkitterick, who, after learning Latin and Greek at fourteen, had taught himself Hebrew by the age of sixteen and could read the whole of the Bible in the original tongue. Ill health interrupted his formal education, and he died at the age of thirty-seven within a year of his appointment. Alexander Brunton then became the Professor of Hebrew from 19 May 1813. It was a progressive time in Edinburgh. Walter Scott received the Freedom of the city; there was talk of a tunnel being built under the Forth to connect the Lothians and Fife, new salt-water baths at Portobello were erected, and a New Town was planned to solve Edinburgh's sanitation problems and the threat of disease.

Elegant, neo-classical boulevards were built in the New Town to attract merchants, academics and lawyers, and soon there were about 15,000 inhabitants there. That it had only one church of the established religion of Scotland was a matter of concern to the ministerial community, but it did not deter the Bruntons from settling there. An unknown young architect, James Craig, was awarded a gold medal and the Freedom of Edinburgh for his winning design for the New Town which incorporated a formal symmetrical grid of single-sided terraces overlooking the old Nor' Loch, now Princes Street Gardens. The Bruntons moved into No. 35 Albany Row (now Albany Street).

Mr B, now 40, saw this as a suitable home for a Professor-elect and his novelist wife. Mary regretted leaving St John Street, and secretly hoped that the New Town would not involve her in an unwelcome social whirl. Their time at St John Street had held literary excitements: the publication of Walter Scott's *Marmion*, in 1808, had, for her, dwarfed many world events, even the jubilee of the accession of King George III, with the ringing of bells, the royal salute from the castle guns, and the warships in Leith Roads which, with the superb firework display, made her think with pride, of her great-uncle Ligonier commanding the military parade at the coronation of this king.

But before moving, the Bruntons decided to go to England

again. Mary wrote to tell her sister-in-law in Orkney, William's wife, Mary, how much she was looking forward to it:

> *You would smile if you knew how bent I am on this journey; and perhaps, with some latent complacency, you would say, "Well, well, I would not give the sight of little Thomas fondling his sister for all the sights of London". But consider, my dear, that I have no Maries or Thomases. When I leave home, I carry all that makes the soul of home with me; I leave nothing behind but walls and furniture; and when I return, I bring back materials for enlivening my fireside.*

There is a touch of wistful longing for children of her own here. She wrote up her holiday experiences in her diary each night at the inn where they stayed. Mr B may have edited these after her death, for it is only his selection of her reminiscences that, as far as we know, remains. He believed that these would be appreciated because (in his words), "they exhibit not only a discriminating love of landscape scenery, but an intelligent observation of the works of art, a patient investigation of subjects which might not have been supposed very much to attract her; a facility for expressing, in brief and perspicuous language, the new ideas which she had acquired".

Mary's diaries are quoted here in the order in which Mr B prepared them for publication:

> *The first entrance to England is far from conveying favourable impressions. The country is bleak and dreary. The road to Belford is abominable. You no sooner cross the boundary, than you are in another kingdom. Near neighbourhood and constant intercourse have effected little intercommunity of manners, language or appearance. Before you advance ten miles on English ground, the women are prettier, the accent is perceptively English, and hats and shoes are universal.*
>
> *The southern part of Yorkshire is a very lovely country. It is certainly too flat; and to Scotch eyes the straight line which the horizon presents is tiresome. But it is divided into innumerable little fields, by hedges in every possible line of curve, and composed*

of whatever can possibly enter into the composition of a hedge, oak, crab, alder, elder, maple, hawthorn, briar, honeysuckle, and a thousand flowering weeds, all blending and unrestrained luxuriance! The English seem to think their hedges entitled to share in the national liberty; for they ramble into every direction, except a straight line; and straggle as they list, without either confining or being confined.

At Doncaster, which is a handsome town, we turned from the great road to see the "Dukeries". Through these parks we drove for nearly a stage; crawling up and lumbering down steep hills, by the vilest roads that ever were seen – for made they are not. We saw nothing which I would have gone a yard to see, except the noble remains of Sherwood Forest. These belong to Thoresby Park; they consist of prodigious oaks, magnificent in decay, flourishing vigorously in the branches, while the trunks are generally hollow. From Ollerton the country continues beautifully swelling and woody to Newark, where we again joined the great road.

A thunderstorm at Grantham forced them to shelter in an inn for the night. When Mary saw what looked like a "new parsonage" nearby she asked the waiter if he could give her the name of the minister, and was astonished that he couldn't. She believed that, as in Scotland, there would be an "intimate and affectionate relationship between pastor and flock".

After the storm passed, they continued:

We were well driven by a good road through Stamford to Burleigh the magnificent! A noble – respectable magnificence! Cecil has as good taste in houses as his mistress had in prime ministers. Admirable pictures! – A Magdalene by Carlo Maratti, Domenicino's mistress, by himself – loveliness personified! Above all, the Salvator Mundi! The features are taken from the letter of Publius, describing the person of Christ. A profusion of curled auburn hair divides on the forehead, and falls to the shoulders. The dark grey eyes are raised in benediction, which the lips are half open to pronounce – one hand holds the sacramental bread; the other is raised in the attitude of devotion. On the table stands the brazen plate, from whence the bread has been lifted; and a cup filled with the emblematic wine. These are the few simple objects which the picture represents. But the magical expression of the countenance! the inimitable execution of every part! Such benevolence – such sensibility – so divine – so touching – cannot be conceived without the soul of Carlo Dolce! How blest must the creature have been whose fancy was peopled with such images!

Arriving in London, they were whisked by a friend from this divine experience to an unexpectedly prosaic oratorio in Covent Garden:

As we are nobody, he advised us to go to the pit, that we might have some chance of seeing and hearing. We were no sooner placed, than the adjoining seats were occupied by some very drunk sailors, and their own true loves, whose expressions of affection made it necessary for us to change our quarters. The music was far superior to anything I had heard before. But in such a place, and in such company, the praise of God seemed almost a blasphemy. All went on peaceably enough, till it pleased Braham, the most delightful singer that ever sung, to sing a nonsensical song about Lord Nelson. Although the words and tune were equally despicable, the song was encored; Braham was engaged elsewhere, and went off without complying. The next performer, Mrs Ashe, a sweet, modest looking creature, whose figure declared her to be in no fit situation to bear fright or ill-usage, tried to begin her song, but was stopped by a tremendous outcry. She tried it again and again, but not a note could be heard, and she desisted. The Halleluiah chorus was begun; but the people bawled, and whistled and hissed, and thumped, and shrieked and groaned, and hooted, and made a thousand indescribable noises besides, till they fairly drowned the organ, the French horns, the kettle-drums, and – the Halleluiah chorus! So I have seen Covent Garden and a row!

If this was a disappointing performance, the visit to St Paul's Cathedral brought some compensation:

Today, the charity children, to the number of 7,000, assembled in St Paul's. They were all clothed in the uniform of their several schools, and their dress was quite new and clean; they were placed on circular seats, rising above each other, under the dome. The area in the centre of the circle which they formed, and the whole of the nave, were filled by many thousand spectators. We had a full view of them all – and indeed I have seen no view so delightful in London as this sight of 7,000 immortal beings, rescued by the charity of their fellow-creatures from ignorance and misery; nor have I heard any music so noble as the burst of their little voices, when the old 100th Psalm rung in the mighty vault of St Paul's. They too sung the Halleluiah chorus, without any accompaniment but the organ. What a contrast to Covent Garden!

After a walk on Hampstead Heath they took an evening drive to Vauxhall:

There was no moon; and from total darkness we at once entered a colonade, blazing with literally thousands of lamps of every various colour, suspended in the forms of festoons, stars, coronets and everything else that is graceful and fantastic. Some of the walks were in total darkness. Others were lighted by a pavilion, or a pagoda, or a temple of lamps to which the walk formed a vista. Several rooms and colonades contained boxes, retreating behind a row of light pillars, twisted round with wreaths of lamps. In each box was laid a table for supper. Bands of music were stationed, and English, Irish, Scotch, German and Turkish airs were performed by musicians in the garb of each country. Many thousands of well-dressed people were assembled in this gay scene. Upon the whole, Vauxhall is the gayest raree show possible – and no bad type of that kind of pleasure, – glittering and bright enough when not too closely examined; but, when seen in the fair day-light, mean, worthless and unsubstantial.

She admired the English countryside, but always with reservations:

Nothing in the beautiful environs of London is so beautiful as the view from Richmond-hill. I do not at all wonder that our Southern neighbours complain of the scarcity of wood in Scotland. The country seen from Richmond-hill is wooded, as far as the eye can reach, like a gentleman's park. All is, to be sure, nearly a dead level. But the multitude of elegant houses – the richness of the woods,– and the windings of the smooth Thames beneath its flat turfy banks, – make the whole scene resemble an immense pleasure ground, interspersed with clumps, lawns, temples and artificial pieces of water. Perhaps my national partialities deceive me, but though I must own we have no prospect so rich; I think we have some infinitely more interesting. There is no compensating for the varied outline of our distant mountains – a dead flat line in the horizon spoils any prospect in my eyes.

The visit to England made Mary more glad than ever that she had resisted her mother's plan to send her to live with her godmother instead of marrying Mr B. England would never have the same appeal for her as Scotland. When she went to see the exhibition of the work of her fellow-countryman, David Wilkie, she thought it "the best bestowed shilling" she had spent in London, loving the colouring in *Picture of a Sick Lady*, finding his *Card-Playing Group* and the *Blind Fiddler* "admirable", but his *Reckoning Day* was, to her, the most exciting.

The visit to the Opera house to hear Catalani sing and Tramezzani act, and watch some dancing "more striking for its agility than its grace", made her comment that "Vestris spins round on one foot an incredible number of times; and he kicks out both before and behind till his leg is perfectly at right angles to his body. But all this kicking and spinning cannot please the sick!" She was beginning to feel terribly tired. "All the pomps and novelties of this world of wonders", she wrote, "become nothing more to me than the shadows that flit along the walls of a prison. Everything tires me now!"

It was not only the demands of their tour that was making her feel exhausted. She was suffering from what Mr B called "an aguish complaint", a kind of fever which was to recur. But it did not halt their progress, and she entered whole-heartedly into their visit to

Woolwich where she was fascinated to watch the making of cannon-balls. There may have been many visitors to Woolwich Arsenal in the early years of the 19th century, but few, if any, young married women who recorded the process in such detail:

> *At Woolwich we saw mountains of balls, and thousands of cannon! We saw the whole process of making ball-cartridges. The balls are cast in a mould, two together, connected by a bar of an inch or two long; they are then cut asunder, close by each ball, and the little bar is thrown back into the melting-pot; then each ball is tied in a rag; then in a paper cone, and the top is fastened down; the cartridges are then packed in small parcels, and the business is finished. Each of these operations is performed by a different hand, and with dispatch almost incredible. One boy fills 4,000 cartridges in a day; little creatures, who could scarcely be entrusted in Orkney with the pastoral care of 3 geese, earn 8 or 9 shillings a week this way.*

They found time to visit Mary's uncle, John Balfour, in his Thames-side luxury home at Charlton. He had then finished his first tour of duty as Member of Parliament for Orkney, and at the age of 63 had no intention of retiring. Mary says nothing about him, but wrote:

> *Charlton is most beautiful; it is almost romantic. The house is very elegant; the windows of a beautiful suite of rooms open out upon a charming little lawn, shaven like green velvet, and bounded in front by an abrupt woody bank, which forms one side of a deep and woody dell. The grounds are sheltered in every direction by woods of various kinds, through which are led walks, as retired as those in Highland glens; yet every opening affords a glimpse of the river, constantly alive with vessels of all sizes, from the gaudy pleasure-boat up to an Indiaman. Of all the places I ever saw, considered merely as a place, Charlton is where I should chuse to set up my rest.*

Next, they toured the Victualling Office at Deptford:

... where I think they told us there were eight stores of beef, one of which we saw containing 16,000 casks, of three hundred weight each. I should have thought there was enough food for a nation. The baking of biscuits going on with astonishing speed; but, as it seemed to me with very bad success. One man kneaded, another shaped, a third divided them, a fourth laid them on a board, and a fifth pushed them into the oven; withal they are ill-shaped and worse fired; some are burnt, and some are raw. This, however, is a little equalised in the drying-rooms which are above pine-apple heat. In the brew-house is a nice little steam-engine by which all the work is performed.

There was one more operational plant – Meux's Brewery – to visit, a brewery which was "as filthy as steam, smoke, dust and rust could make it", except for the steam-engine which was "as clean as the bars of a dining-room grate":

The first operation of this engine is to stir the malt in vats of 28 feet in diameter, filled with boiling water; the second is, in due time, to raise the wort to the coolers in the floor above; then this wort is conveyed by leaden pipes into the tub where it is to ferment, and afterwards into the casks where the porter is first deposited. One of these casks, which I saw, measures seventy feet in diameter, and is said to have cost £10,000; the iron hoops on it weigh 80 tons; and we were told that it actually contained, when we saw it, 18,000 barrels, or £40,000 worth of porter. Another contained 16,000 barrels, and from thence to 4,000; there are about seventy casks in the store. From the top of this immense building, which holds this vast apparatus, we had a complete view of London and the adjacent country. I must own, however, that I was rejoiced to find myself once more safe in the street. I believe, indeed, that I am, as Dr Blair phrases it, "destined to creep through the inferior walks of life"; for I never feel myself in a very elevated position without being seized with an universal tremor. I shook in every limb after coming down.

A tour of England in the early 19th century probably took in almost as many of the show-places which attract visitors today.

Windsor, Blenheim, Oxford, Stratford and Warwick were on the list. Windsor had a special appeal:

It makes a very noble appearance as it rises above the woods with its banners floating in the air. It is indeed the only royal residence I have seen at all fit for a king. The apartments are very handsome – and the Hanoverian plate superb. There are some very fine pictures. I was particularly struck with two small ones by Carlo Dolce – a Madonna – and a "Bearing the Cross". The first is finished exquisitely; the face is lovely, and the drapery perfectly graceful. The deep sorrow in the face of the Saviour is wonderfully touching; the hands are inimitable. These are in the king's dressing closet. In the same room is a beautiful sketch by Rubens. In the king's drawing-room is a "Holy Family", the most interesting of any of Rubens' pictures which I have seen. "Venus attired by the Graces", by Guido, seems a master-piece of grace and nature. However, as gentlemen are admitted to her Godess-ship's presence, I wish her tire-women had been a little more expeditious. The apartments immediately over those occupied by the king are shut up; nor is anyone allowed to walk beneath his windows. We saw his private chapel, where he was accustomed to attend regularly every day with his family; but the good man's seat has long been vacant, and it will be long before his equal fills it. From the top of the round tower there is a very rich and extensive view; but, except on the Eton side, still less interesting than Richmond-hill.

When the itinerary took them to Oxford, Blenheim, Woodstock, Stratford-on-Avon and Warwick, there was such a glory of experience for Mary that her enjoyment overflowed:

From Windsor we went by Henley to Oxford, through one of the loveliest countries upon earth. The ground is actually hilly. Every spot is cultivated, or richly wooded, the fields bear fine crops, in spite of farming vile beyond expression; and the whole is clothed with the brightest verdure imaginable. Nothing is more striking, in a comparison of the two extremities of the island, than the difference of colour. Even our richest fields in Scotland have either a brown or a greyish cast; and except upon a gentleman's lawn, the verdure of English grass is never seen to the north of Newcastle. The approach to Oxford is very striking. The spires are seen at a distance, mingling with trees; which are fine, in spite of the barbarous custom of lopping their lower branches. As you enter the town, Magdalene College is the first thing you see. As you proceed along the High Street, something new and grand presents itself at every step; spires, domes, minarets and arches! I have seen no street of the same length at all comparable to fit it for magnificence. It bends a little, so that something is always left to expectation. We quickly procured a guide who conducted us to the Chapel of Magdalene. One end of the chapel contains a window, painted in so elegant a design that I could scarcely believe its antiquity. The side windows in the choir are in the same style of colouring and unfortunately darken the altar-piece, a most glorious picture! It represents the Saviour bending under his cross; his temples bleeding with the thorns. The attitude is a wonderful mixture of grace and exhaustion; the countenance expresses the noblest resignation. The drapery is very fine; not frittered away in small lights and shadows, but disposed in grand broad folds, the colour harmoniously sober – the finishing perfect, – a drop of blood has trickled down to the neck, – every muscle in the feet, every vein in the hand is perceptible. The walks of Magdalene College are shadowed by tall trees, and lie along the banks of the Cherwell; a stream which will never disturb the students' musings, either by its noise or motion. Our guide told us that the walks were always cool, because of a pleasant hair which came from the water. He made us particularly notice "Haddison's walk – the great poet as wrote the Spectators".

The Radcliffe Library is a very beautiful Rotunda, with a gallery running round it. As to books, there are none except a few medical ones.

The Pomfret Marbles are old patched remnants – bodies without heads, and heads without bodies. Some of these scraps are very fine, but most of them spoiled by modern mending. From the Marbles we went to the Theatre – that is, the place where disputations are held. It is a room above eighty feet long, and above seventy broad; the largest roof, we were told, in the kingdom, unsupported by pillars. The roof is made of square pieces of wood, all joined together by screws and nuts. The room is said to contain 5,000 persons, which appears to me incredible. There are galleries on three sides. I am disappointed in the Theatre, which is far inferior to the Radcliffe, both in magnificence and beauty . . . The gardens at St. John's are very pretty; and kept, like everything about Oxford, with exemplary neatness.

Though I am absolutely tired of looking at pictures, we went with new pleasure to take a second view of the altar-piece of the Magdalene Chapel. Next to the Burleigh Carlo Dolce, it is the most enchanting picture I ever saw. I must not pretend to judge, but, if it be a Guido, it is finished in a manner differing from his ordinary style. It seems to have roused the enthusiasm of the woman who shews it. She pointed out its beauties with the warmest and most naif admiration. "Oh! Madam!", she said to me with tears in her eyes, "What do you think? I have shown this glorious picture for thirty years, and now I must leave it. I buried my husband six weeks ago, and the shewing of them things is always given to men. But, thank God, they cannot hinder me from seeing it in the time of prayers". She was delighted with our admiration, and positively refused a fee at parting!!! We returned to the "Angel" to dinner, and then left this most interesting and (if I may except "mine own romantic town") most beautiful city that ever I beheld.

****

I was disappointed in the first coup d'oeil of Blenheim. I had heard too much of it. The water was full of weeds, betraying at once its artificial origin. The poorest rill that tosses in its rocky channel, or frets against the pebbles which it has borne down the hill, is less admirable indeed, but more interesting, than an ocean which we know to be confined by man's devices. But Blenheim is intended to astonish, not to interest. It is a huge splendid show-box, made to be looked at, and only to be looked at. The house is princely; but the moment you enter it you perceive that it is of no more use to the owner than its picture would be. He may shew – but he cannot live in it. In fact, a very small part of it is in family use. The rest, for payment of certain most unreasonable fees, is at the service of the public. The entrance has magnificence; the saloon too is superb; (with fine marble portals). The Library is splendid – pillars, pilasters and basement of marble, but ill-proportioned, and not very fully lighted. The chapel is "very well", with a princely monument to "the Duke". The other apartments are well enough. There are some fine pictures – a large collection of Rubenses. A fine Rembrandt – "Isaac blessing Jacob" – two beggar boys by Murillo; a Madonna by Carlo Dolce – most delightful. We bought the Blenheim Guide by Dr. Mavor. The China Gallery has 2,000 year-old-porcelain – but utterly void of beauty or interest to me. I paid one half-crown to see it; I would not give another for the whole collection. In one of the attached offices is the Titian gallery, hung, I cannot say ornamented, with pictures by that master. They represent about a score of gods and godesses as large as life and as ugly as sin. I wish, on the other hand, that sin were always as naked as they. Nobody could then be deceived about its nature . . . The park is truly fine.

We escaped from Woodstock; and, with the worst driving we have ever seen since we left home, reached Stratford-on-Avon before it was quite dark. We hurried to Shakespeare's house – sat in his chair – saw his bedroom – the room where he was born! The walls are covered with names of such as wished to buy a part of his immortality at a cheap rate. Part of his furniture remains; but all is falling fast to decay.

Next morning, we went by an admirable road, through a pretty country, to Warwick. Warwick has been a fortified town. It still has a portcullis and a tower at each end. It is clean, handsome, and remarkably well paved. The avenue to the castle is strikingly appropriate. It is a winding road cut through solid rock, which rises on each side to the height of twelve or fifteen feet, and is crowned with ivy and tangled shrubs. The great court of the castle is admirable. Here is nothing that calls you to admire with the annoyance of upstart finery; but there is a magnificence more touching than splendour – the sober dignity of baronial pomp softened by the hand of time into something between beauty and sublimity. The stately towers and battlement; unshaken by the storms of ages, are here and there gracefully shrouded in ivy.

There is a reality – a consistency – an air of nature, I may say, in the majesty of Warwick, which gives it a most interesting charm. To this charm the Prince of Wales alluded very happily, when he said to someone who compared Warwick with Blenheim, "we can build a Blenheim". Three sides of the court are surrounded by the buildings connected with the castle. The fourth is occupied by what has once been a fortified embankment, but it is now thickly covered with trees, evergreens, and flowering shrubs. Close under the walls of the castle flows the Avon, which is here a very beautiful stream; and from some of the Gothic windows there is a most appropriate view of the ruined arches of a bridge, which once commanded the fortress. The entrance hall of Warwick is not so superb as that of Blenheim; but it is more unaffected. It is characteristically ornamented with arms, furs of animals, and antlers of the Moose Deer. It is lined with oak, and is, as well as the very long and noble suite of apartments into which it opens, finished in the style of Henry VII's time. One of the largest rooms in the house is panelled with carved cedar. The gardens are fine and extensive. The dressed ground commands beautiful glimpses of the park and the adjacent country. In the Conservatory is the superb Warwick vase. It was found in Herculaneum, and has been transported without injury. It is made from one block of pure white marble; the carving is in alto relievo, and as fresh as if it has been cut yesterday. We were told that it contains 120 gallons . . .

The Scottish painter, Gavin Hamilton, excavated the fragments of marble which made up the vase when working beside Hadrian's Villa, about 15 miles east of Rome. He got £300 of financial help for its reconstruction from a fellow-Scot Sir William Hamilton, the British Envoy Extraordinary to the Court of Naples, and in 1778 Sir William's nephew George, second Earl of Warwick, placed it in the courtyard of Warwick Castle. Two hundred years later it was sold to London dealers who sold it to the Metropolitan Museum of Art in New York. When the granting of an export licence was deferred, a purchase price of £253,808 was raised by the Burrell Collection, the Scottish Heritage Fund, the National Art-Collections Fund, and two charities which remain anonymous. Described as "the finest vase in the world", it is simply, yet dramatically displayed in the Burrell Collection in Glasgow. I have not read anywhere, except in Mary's account, that its capacity is 120 gallons.

The return to Edinburgh was via Harrogate, and Mary pronounced the holiday "on the whole, most delightful".

Settled in the New Town, and feeling confident after the successful reception of *Self-Control*, Mary was ready to start writing again. Mr B suggested that she could continue the plan she had started in her first novel, this time showing how, when *Self-Control* has been neglected, the mind must be controlled by suffering before it can, "hope for usefulness and true enjoyment". With reservations, she agreed, and towards the end of 1812, *Discipline*, was begun. She tried to draw up a synopsis on his advice, but discarded it when he thought it a little too "meagre". (See Appendix.)

She convinced herself that it was tiredness after their holiday that made her write more laboriously this time. By the end of November 1812 she told Mrs Izett that Ellen (her new heroine) "comes on slowly, but she will do better by and by if I can adhere to my resolution of writing a little every day". In her dedication to Christianity she was convinced that what she called her "stock of wits" were "under the management and control of a higher power" to which she believed the success of *Self-Control* was due. She mentioned this to Mrs Izett:

> *You will answer, "Have you not long thought so?" Yes, I have long believed it, but now I feel it. Do you not see the difference? Either by his own operations on the soul, or by his providence in ordering matters over which we have no controul, he rules our understanding – our will – our conscience – our belief. Oh! then how zealous ought we to be in asking direction, since he can afford it in such a variety of ways; and since circumstances, which to us appear as trivial as the sport of flies, may by him be made to accomplish his promise, that all shall work together for good to them who love him. You see to whom the success of Self-Control was owing. I hope I may lawfully ask a blessing for this thing also! It would be sinful to enter upon a work of years, which was so trivial, or useless, or unlawful, that I could not ask a blessing for*

it. But, if I do ask one, it will be a manifest absurdity to trifle over my employment. The other began as pastime. This has been work from the beginning. I find that the serious style best suits my talent and my inclination. I hope, therefore, that when I come to the serious part of the book, I shall proceed with more ease and pleasure. It is not far off now.

The story of *Discipline* is based on the fortunes of the beautiful and wealthy Ellen Percy who undergoes a frustrated elopement, bereavement, perjury, and a period in a madhouse before eventually finding happiness in Scotland. The busy Mrs Izett accused Mary, in a friendly way, of apathy, but Mary was too fond of her old friend to take offence:

You give me a pretty broad hint, that my little interest in my present work proceeds from my own indolence. To this I can make an answer, which satisfies myself. I can, and often do, write when I would rather let it alone. But in these circumstances I never write well, nor can I by any exertion write better. The only fruit of my endeavours is strong disgust at the whole. An author can no more invent, who is not 'i' the vein', than a painter could draw a straight line whose hand was in the tremor of an ague-fit. To tell me that I am idle, is only Pharaoh's call for bricks without straw.

There was a difference between the writing of *Self-Control,* when Mary found she had little time for anything else, and *Discipline,* when, in the words of Mr B she usually had, "some female work going on" and, "in the intervals of sewing and knotting she wrote down what she had first deliberately considered both in regard to sentiment and style".

The theme of the book is the reformation of character through hardship and suffering, many of the characters and events once again being drawn from life. There is an elopement, but the man involved is not a Presbyterian minister like Mr B, but a cad who opts out of it on learning that his future father-in-law is bankrupt and his bride-to-be no longer an heiress. But the hero, a Presbyterian, with a home in Scotland, eventually wins the lady's hand. Mary found it difficult to find material and characters that were not repetitive – not to make Ellen's father, on the verge of bankruptcy, too much like de Montreville in *Self-Control*, nor to make the hardships that Ellen suffered too much like Laura's.

Although the plots of both books have such wild oscillations of fortune, outrageous coincidences, and threats to the sanity of the heroines, this is designed to cloak the moral message so as to excite the interest of those readers Mary most wished to reach. Impressed by the success Maria Edgeworth had in the localising of a story, a success which had not escaped the notice of the young Walter Scott when he began to present Scotland and its history to the world in the form of fiction, Mary decided to move the activity in the third volume of *Discipline* to the Highlands to give the book added popularity, never realising that this would cause her much distress before she was finally persuaded to keep it in.

The quotation on the title page of *Discipline* is from Joanna Baillie:

All pitying Heaven,
Severe in mercy, chastening in its love,
Ofttimes in dark and awful visitation
Doth interpose; and leads the wanderer back
To the straight path.

Mary wrote to her the autumn of 1813 to tell her about her summer holiday in Perthshire, with no mention of *Discipline*:

. . . many a pleasant ramble had I! One of them was to Killivrochan, the wildest of all human habitations. It stands upon the banks of the Tummel, about two miles (Highland miles perhaps) above the pass of Killiecrankie. Did you ever see the Tummel? It is the stream of my affection! Of all rivers it is the most truly Highland; an impetuous melancholy, romantic stream, foaming among the fragments that have fallen from mountains which seem to have been cleft for its course. Killivrochan has no lawns nor gardens near it; no paltry work of man's device, to fritter away the majesty of nature! Fortunately there is no room for such disfigurements; for the site of the house

occupies the only level spot between a perpendicular mountain and the river . . .

There seemed less spare time now. The Bruntons' circle of friends had widened "unmercifully", and although Mary could now mix on an equal footing with people "eminent for talents and respectability" she missed having more opportunities for dozing by her own fireside or wandering out unnoticed in the town. But she always made time to keep in touch with Orkney, and wrote to Aunt Craigie who had heard rumours that her niece was an authoress:

William has probably told you what a busy woman I am. If anybody had told me three years ago, that, even to my brother, I should ever boldly avow myself an author, I would have fearlessly asserted the thing to be impossible; and if, before Self-Control went to press, I could have guessed that it would be traced to me, I would certainly have put it on the fire . . . I never absolutely denied it, indeed; for that would have been a direct falsehood; but I always thought myself at liberty to mislead those who wanted the delicacy which has prevented you from questioning me on the subject . . .

William took more than a casual interest in her writing. They had an affectionate relationship – he told her about his children, and she invited his criticism of her work. Once, when he thought that his son, Thomas (3), was not growing fast enough, she replied:

As to the size of your little gentleman, you must reconcile yourself to that, by hoping that, like you, like Caesar, Alexander the Great, myself and others, our friend may hide a capacious soul in a diminutive body . . . While you are so much occupied with your own brat, I thank you for taking such an interest in mine. In one respect, yours has the advantage; for, while he would thrive although I were to forget his very existence, mine depends not a little upon the interest you take in her for her growth and progress. She will come on much better for the mention you make of her. No fear of the falls of Niagara! Ellen is too common-place a person for such achievements; and none of her future adventures are at all more surprising than those which I read to you. Only two dangers now threaten her; the one is, that I may give up recording such a humble history; the other, that after I have done my best, it may be little read. To be sure, what satisfies you may well content the herd of novel-readers. But it is a very different thing to hear a manuscript read, from sitting down with a printed book in one's hand to spy faults; or from seeking amusement, without any reference to the author or to the judgment which one's friends form of the work. Even I think Self-Control in print a far worse performance than Self-Control in manuscript. However, I mean to do my best for my second daughter; and if I live and thrive till this time next year, we shall see how she looks in "wire-wove and hot-pressed".

Writing in the peace and quiet of St. Leonard's, she told William that it would be a place to his heart's content – "so buried from the view of all earthly things and personal!" By the end of 1814, she reckoned that six weeks of hard work would finish the manuscript of *Discipline,* allowing time for corrections. "When I have ended", she said, "I will dance on top of it, as the man in the song was to do with his dead wife. I am sure she was not half such a plague to him as my book has been to me".

She had enjoyed writing the adventures of Ellen Percy in the Highlands more than any other part of the book because she felt herself on home ground, and was completely unprepared for the effect which the publication of Walter Scott's new novel *Waverley* would have on her. Mr B described her reaction:

It came into her hands while she was in the country, ignorant of its plan, or of its claim to regard; she was so fascinated by it that she sat up till she had finished the reading of the whole. Her anticipation of its success was, from the first, confident and unhesitating. With the honest buoyancy of a kindred spirit she exulted in the prospect of the author's fame; and, in rejoicing that a favourite object had been accomplished so admirably, forgot how much the plan interfered with her own. When this view of the subject struck her, with all the native openness of her mind, she felt and acknowledged her own inferiority. Not from disappointment or ill-humour, but from pure and unaffected humility, she resolved at first to cancel the Highland part of her story altogether. I could not agree to the sacrifice. I endeavoured to convince her that the bias which Waverley would give to the public taste might rather prove favourable to her plan, that public curiosity would be roused by what the great master had done; that the sketches of a different observer, finished in a very different style, and taken from an entirely different point of view, would only be more attractive because attention had previously been directed to the subject.

Eventually, Mary saw the wisdom of Mr B's arguments and was persuaded to retain the Highland episode. But she had lost a certain amount of confidence and returned to her writing more slowly than before, finishing it, according to Mr B, "with far less both of spirit and hope than attended the tracing of the original design". On 15 August 1814, she wrote to Mrs Izett again:

Ellen is at an end. She was finished at three o'clock this morning, and I waked Mr B out of his first sleep to hear of her wedding. I am correcting; which is not the part of the business the most to my liking. I have a great aversion to blot a page of good clean writing.
If no accident befall – if my manuscript is neither burnt, nor stolen nor lost, – perhaps the book will be in your hands before Christmas. I dare say you will make a pause in your historical course to read it – were it only to see how . . . will like it: and if she ventures at all to disapprove, you will colour up to the ears, and have just enough self-command to hold your tongue.
Have you finished Waverley? And what think you of the scenes at Carlisle? Are they not admirable? I assure you, that in my opinion they are absolutely matchless for nature, character, originality and pathos. Flora's "seam", and the "paper-coronet" are themselves worth whole volumes of common inventions. And what think you of Evan's speech? It delights my very soul. Why should an epic or a tragedy be supposed to hold such an exalted place in composition, while a novel is almost a nickname

for a book? Does not a novel admit of as noble sentiments – as lively description – as natural character – as perfect unity of action – and a moral as irresistable as either of them? I protest, I think a fiction containing a just representation of human beings and of their actions – a connected, interesting and probable story, conducting to a useful and impressive moral lesson – might be one of the greatest efforts of human genius. Let the admirable construction of fable in Tom Jones be employed to unfold characters like Miss Edgworth's – let it be told with the eloquence of Rousseau, and with the simplicity of Goldsmith – let it be all this, and Milton need not have been ashamed of the work! But novels have got an ill name, therefore "give the novels to the dogs". I have done with them, for if even the best possible could be comparatively despised, what is to become of mine? Well! What shall I do next? Give me your advice; and, if I like it, I will take it.

****

I began the Gaelic Grammar y'day. The pronunciation is terribly unintelligible. "There is no sound like this in English" is a very spirit-breaking index. I fear I shall never make out the true croaking and spluttering. If I persevere, however, I may astonish you when we meet – shocking your ears with your dear native tongue spoken in the barbarous accents of a southron. But to what purpose should I persevere?

Discipline was published on 13 December 1814, and, like *Self-Control,* was printed from the first copy by George Ramsay & Co., for Manners & Miller, Edinburgh. "It is very unfortunate in coming after *Waverley*", Mary wrote to Aunt Craigie, "by far the most splendid exhibition of talent in the novel way which has appeared since the days of Fielding and Smollet . . . What a competitor for poor little me! The worst of it all is, that I have ventured unconsciously on Waverley's own ground, by carrying my heroine to the Highlands! . . . In authorship luck does a great deal. *Self-Control* was more successful than many a better book has been".

Discipline was another overnight success, extending to 476 pages with a carefully selected verse to head each of the 30 chapters, chosen from 20 different poets including Byron, Cowper, Crabbe, Goldsmith, Gray, Scott and Shakespeare. Although relieved to see it in print at last, Mary did not experience the same sense of excitement that she had felt over *Self-Control.* Mr B described how she felt:

> *The honied words of praise were never valuable to her. They had now lost the charm of novelty, and she doubted whether they retained the more valuable recommendation of truth. Her standard for estimating the skill in the delineation of character had been raised by the appearance of Waverley; and she felt – more perhaps than she ought to have done – how poorly her own sketches appeared beside those of that masterly work. The silence too, of the principal literary journals, discouraged her. She had never, indeed, expected to attract much of their notice; but, while other works of the same kind were discussed in their pages, she thought that if they had judged favourably as to the usefulness of her labours, they would not have withheld from her their advice and encouragement.*

Four days after the publication of *Discipline,* Mr B was awarded the degree of Doctor of Divinity (Edinburgh) on 17 December 1814.

Unable to throw off her sense of guilt for treading the same ground as Walter Scott, Mary wrote a long, explanatory introduction to *Discipline* which is included in the Appendix to this volume.

William sent his comments after reading the book, and Mary replied:

> *I thank you for your criticisms: some of them have served the purpose for which I presume you intended them, by making me laugh heartily. Not but I acknowledge there is some justice in them all, except in your attack upon my Scotchman; who, I assure you, is not so very marble, but that he is in high favour with the ladies. A handsome, fashionable young one, the other day, embargoed Mr Miller in a corner of his own shop, till he should tell her who Mr Maitland was; since, "beyond all doubt, the*

> *character was a real one". As for the Highlands, you know they are quite the rage. All the novel-reading misses have seen and admired them in the verdure and sunshine of July. Now, what novel-reading miss ever had common sense enough to doubt that what is pleasing to the eye, should be desirable in possession; or that what charms for an evening, should delight for ever? As for my religion, I allow that there is too much for an amusement, perhaps for good taste; nevertheless, I cannot bate you one iota. For the great purpose of the book is to procure admission for the religion of a sound mind of the Bible, where it cannot find access in any other form. Yes! I say the great purpose; for, though I love money dearly, money is not my motive for writing as I do; nor for the complexion and sentiments of my books. On the contrary, I am quite sure I might make twice as much of my labour if I could bring myself to present to the public an easy and flexible sort of virtue – possessing no strong support, and being, indeed, too light to need any – instead of the old-fashioned erect morality which "falls not, because it is founded on a rock?"*

By the age of thirty, William was a fair critic, not afraid of telling his sister that had she been free of her determinedly useful, but, to his mind, restrictive aim of imparting morality to her readers, she could have become a best-selling novelist of quite a different kind. Sometimes he tried his hand at writing too.

The repairing of the Tron Church in the summer of 1815, gave Mr B the chance of another holiday and he and Mary decided to go to England again. Initially, Mary was very tired, and of all the "1,000 things" which they saw at the Art Exhibition at Somerset House, the only picture which she could remember to record in her diary was David Wilkie's *Distraining for Rent* – "superior in expression and moral effect as it is inferior in finishing to the best works of Mieris and Gerard Dow; but then, such labour to paint cabbages and carrots! It would be far easier to raise them, and of far more use". A very practical observation from the girl who grew up on an Orkney farm.

They went by boat to Kew Gardens, returning to Richmond to climb the hill and look at the view. Mary thought it "the richest possible", and "very beautiful", but decided it was only the river that made it so. They saw a glorious sunset which threw, in her words, "a fine pillar of light along the river, and afterwards tinged it with the richest shades of orange, fading, as we approached the boat, to silver. The water, an unruffled mirror, reflected every tree or cloud, and, as it grew dark, transformed every taper on the banks into a slender shaft of fire. We landed about ten after a very pleasant excursion".

At the National School next day she was allowed to take her place in the lowest class and say the lesson with the children, watching them learning to make their letters in sand, and form syllables:

> *... the first girl calls out 'a'; after an interval sufficient to count to six, the second calls 'b'; after a like interval, the third calls out 'ab', etc. If any girl does not know the letter or syllable which it is her turn to say, the next is tried, and the first who can say, takes the place of all who cannot. If any girl is observed trifling, she is instantly called on. In the highest class, the children read selections from the Scriptures; and, in addition to the other exercises, are examined ... on the meaning of what they read. Nothing can be more striking than the eagerness of attention which the children show, although no other punishment is inflicted for idleness than loss of place in class. The lowest class being found the most difficult to train, the best teacher is reserved for it. The mistress goes continually from class to class, speaking to the children, reproving or applauding them by name.*

Salisbury was disappointing – rather dirty and shabby, Mary said, with "a ditch called a canal in each street" which provided the town with fairly clean water. The cathedral, in an open square, was surrounded by trees and gravel walks. Mary was disappointed that the 400ft spire, "built without perforations" was quite plain. She would have been happier with a little more grandeur – but the interior made up for what the exterior lacked:

> *The altar stands in a beautiful little chapel, into which the church is opened. Some of its pillars are wonderfully light, not more than a foot in diameter. Others are composed of clusters of*

still more slender shafts united to each other only by the capital. The pillars of the nave and choir are also clustered. All the windows are alike and of the simplest structure, each consisting of three plain Gothic arches. That over the West door is stained, the one behind the altar is stained also. It contains only one figure, and represents the resurrection of our Saviour. The side windows being of common glass, the church is glaringly light; and it is all as clean as possible. The Chapter House somewhat resembles that of York, except that the roof is supported by a slender pillar in the centre. It is so light that when approaching it through the cloisters I thought the roof was gone. The whole is inferior to York Minster.

Hampshire was their next stopping-place and they found the countryside round Southampton very beautiful. Taken by water to the 16th-century ruins of Netley Abbey, roofless, with part of the church and its east window still standing, Mary found the beauty of its antiquity so compelling that she reached for her sketchbook, only to be frustrated by a party of English tourists "preceded by baskets of meat and drink" who took the place over, accompanied by a regimental band with kettle-drums. This, and the stalls selling toys and gingerbread at the entrance to the Abbey, aroused her to anger when she realised that even the sheltering woods and the lonely situation were no protection for a monument of such ancient and historic beauty.

The furthest south that they travelled was to the Isle of Wight where, at Newport, they walked up to a "signal-post" to get a view of what they expected to be the garden of England but instead found themselves overlooking "an ugly, bare heath . . . dull heights and uninteresting hollows". Ventnor was no better. The inn, where Mary wrote up her diary, though comfortable, was as expensive as a London hotel.

The landscape . . . consists of bare ugly hills, dreary open sea, and crags as regular in shape, and strata as a wall. Bonchurch is pretty and very rugged. Perhaps the good folks may think it sublime who never saw any hill higher than Ludgate, or any rocks larger than those in a pavement. The cottages are beautiful.

One of the poorest had a fig-tree, a passion flower and a myrtle, on the front of it. Many have vines; but this is universal since we left London. The people in the Isle of Wight are unlike any other English. Ill-looking, swarthy, generally black-eyed. The children are dirty and ragged . . . Except round the villas or hamlets the country is entirely bare, or its few trees stunted or cankered. In short, it is not worth a Scotsman's trouble to cross a ferry of five miles in order to see a country like his own, but every way inferior, bare as East Lothian, without being rich; only rough where it pretends to be magnificent, and merely dull where it affects the sublime. The dialect is very nearly unintelligible, but in answer to almost every question, we can make out "I don't know". A Scotch militiaman, whom we met near Niton says, "They are the most ignorant brutes that ever were made. You may sit in a public house madam, a whole day, and never hear a word of edification, farther than what farmer has the fattest calf".

The militiaman was equally forthright when they all had what Mary described as "a sad scramble" from Niton to a new medicinal spring close by. He lost no time in saying that "one drink of Pitcaithly is worth the whole well" – a remark which was probably lost on the local inhabitants who were unaware of the fame of the Pitcaithly wells in Perthshire for their medicinal properties.

Mary thought Cowes and Ride (sic) were the prettiest places on the Isle of Wight. After a fairly good crossing to Portsmouth 'with some sea and no wind', she walked round the ramparts and made her observations:

Portsmouth is a regular fortification. Next to the town there is a high mound of earth – the rampart. Upon this brick wall, from the top the earthwork slopes outward, and is covered and coped with turf – the curtain. This weakens the force of the balls, which lodge in it rather than rebound, and prevent splintering. Beyond this, at the bottom of the curtain, a low wall. Then comes the fosse – a ditch of great length, which can be filled with sea-water in a moment by sluices. On the outer edge is the covered way; a wall with a pallisade on the inside from which the musquetry might play. Without this again is the glacis; a field of considerable breadth, sloped at such an angle so that a ball rebounding from it would not touch the works. At regular intervals the curtain is broken by bastions. These are angular projections, so placed that should an enemy get within the outworks, the side guns from these bastions would rake them, which is called enflading. Most of the guns, being placed in niches made for them through the curtain, can fire in only one direction. This disadvantage is balanced by the protection the curtain gives to the artillerymen. But some of the guns are placed en barbette, that is, on top of the curtain where they can be aimed at pleasure, but where the men are quite exposed. The ramparts are planted with trees, which prevent the enemy from taking aim at particular buildings, and serve also by their roots to bind the earth in the rampart. The opposite side of the harbour is defended by fortifications at Gosport, and farther inland, Portsea also is completely fortified. Lastly, the whole "island" is defended on the land side by strong lines and double moats.

These detailed notes in Mary's diary on the fortifications of an English sea-port were probably made so that she could discuss them logically with William on her return, in the same way as the subject of her next entry:

We went aboard the Nelson, which though afloat has neither crew nor rigging. She is quite new. She measures 2400 feet from stem to stern. [The *Nelson* is in fact a little over 200 feet long]. *She rates at 2800 tons of ballast on board; about half of this will be thrown out to make way for the guns. There is something awful in the size and strength of everything around you as you stand between decks; but the interest is much lessened by her wanting her stores, rigging and crew. She is at present only three shabby galleries of prodigious length.*

Brighton, after visiting a "block manufactory", and travelling through "frightful country" and over bad roads, did not satisfy any feeling of joyous anticipation that there might have been:

The consummation of deformity; a brick town, crammed into a hollow between two naked hills, open only towards the sea. Not one spire breaks the dullness of the red roofs, nor one tree the sameness of the downs; nor one point the dreariness of the ocean. O what a contrast to the neighbourhood of Bath! Immediately on leaving Brighton the country improves and soon becomes quite beautiful. At first it is hilly, afterwards agreeably swelling; everywhere fertile and extremely woody. The trees are chiefly oak, and there are many very fine. Tilgate forest consists of small birch coppice. The soil near the coast is chalky . . . The commons are more numerous as you approach London, but of no great interest . . . The villas seem encroaching in all directions.

They left London on Tuesday, 25 July 1815, and Mary felt no great wish to visit it again, more on account of the people she'd met there than what she'd actually seen. Apart from thinking that their features were less strongly marked than those of her own countrymen, she felt at a disadvantage by only seeing them in drawing-rooms, "and a drawing-room, like the grave", she said, "effaces all distinctions". There always seemed to be a set of topics from which no-one thought of departing – all taking the same views, or lining up their views with those of their own class. If you knew anyone's birth, profession and place of worship, you could guess what their moral, political and religious opinions would be. She felt very ill at ease in this kind of company.

Harvesting was going on in the fields on their way to Oxford, but it seemed a less cheerful occasion than in Scotland. No band of reapers – "nae daffing, nae gabbing", Mary wrote, and was astonished to see in one fine field of wheat one man cutting at one corner, and one woman at another.

She felt more at home here in Oxford and eager to go to Magdalene College to see the Carlo Dolce altarpiece again. Hoping to renew acquaintance with the woman who had previously been their guide, she met her son who had made his fortune in India and returned to look after his mother. "A man", she wrote in her diary, "shows the picture now, with great sang-froid". She could detect in the picture the style of the 16th-17th century Italian painter Guido Reni of the Bolognese School who, like the Caracci brothers, was among its most distinguished artists. Emotionally, she found the visits to Magdalene College the most rewarding of this English tour.

As their journey progressed, she found herself comparing the English and the Scottish countryside:

> *The English villas repose on velvet lawns which the giant oak and luxuriant chestnut dapple with their broad shadows. Ours stand square and ungraceful on benty fields, inclosed by parallelograms of firs; but ours are tenanted by their owners, and the best feelings and principles of human nature find exercise there; while the villas of England are either altogether deserted, or inhabited by menials and land stewards. Our fields boast no beauty, either of form or colour; but they are at once frugally cultivated and every year makes new encroachments on the barren-ness of nature. Our cottages range in vile rows, flanked with pig-styes and fronted with dunghills, but our cottagers have Bibles, and can read them; they are poor, but not paupers. In some of the agricultural parishes of England we found more than half the population receiving charity (if I may prostitute the word) from the remainder. Every mile in Scotland shows you new houses, new fields, new plantations. In England, everything is old; and this is one great cause of its beauty – trees, grass, cottages, all are in maturity, if not in decay. The first young plantation of any extent which I observed in England was on the borders of the New Forest; and in the southern counties, I scarcely saw one new cottage, unless in the neighbourhood of large towns.*

It was vacation time in Oxford, so they were able to walk quietly in the gardens of the colleges before going on to Witney, of blanket-making fame, and then to Northleach where Mary made a quick sketch of the curious old church with its splendidly carved south porch, one of the finest examples of the churches built by the old wool-merchants, and a tourist attraction in the little stone-built town which was once a centre of the Cotswold woollen trade.

Now they had the prospect of seventeen days rest and "pleasant idleness" at Cheltenham after travelling there over "bare, cold, ugly country", seeing the Malvern hills, which Mary thought strongly resembled the best aspect of the Pentlands. She liked the neatness of Cheltenham, the mile-long town, surrounded by villas and cottages, green fields and hedgerows, and was especially delighted with the Vale of Evesham with its snug cottages, orchards, village-churches, shady lanes and fields "green as the first spring of Eden". Almost every cottage looked picturesque, "mantled with a vine" and with a little court of flowers in front of it. At Cheltenham there is, for the first time in Mary's diary of the itinerary, a glimpse of their daily routine:

> *Between seven and nine in the morning we all contrive to walk half a mile to the well, and drink an English pint or two of salt water. From nine to eleven, breakfast is on the table, and everyone drops in at his own convenience to partake. Then each "strolls off his glad way" in this Castle of Indolence. Those who have a carriage drive backward and forward in the street. This saves the sixpence which the gate would cost, and thus they can better afford to stop at an auction, and buy twenty pounds worth of trash, which they do not want. At five, we meet for dinner, – dressed, but not fine. – After tea, the libraries, the theatre, the concert-room, the gaming-houses, are open for those who chuse them; and there are lights in the drawing-room for workers and readers. In every direction the walks and rides are delightful. There are hills at no great distance, on three sides of the town; and from every little eminence there are new views of this magnificent valley.*

Next, they set out for Ross. The beauty of the Wye Valley completely enchanted Mary and was to stay in her memory longer than any other landscape she had seen on this English journey. For that reason, Mr B made a point of retaining the long descriptive passages of it that she made:

> *The road is hilly and beautiful. It enters the high country about seven miles from Gloucester; and winds on among rich narrow dells, and hills cultivated and peopled to the summit. The last circumstance distinguishes this country from Scotland; as do also numerous orchards, and dells without a brook. Longhope and Lea*

are sweet villages – pictures of seclusion and repose! Ross is a very shabby old town, in a pretty situation, looking down from a high bank on the Wye. The river was at this season too shallow for sailing. The stage to Monmouth seems to be much finer than that of Ross. It lies in the bottom of a beautiful basin, formed by steep woody hills, all in the highest stage of cultivation. Up to the very top of these, the little white cottages peep from among their thickets and orchards. The country is divided into baby farms, and peopled with labouring tenants and this gives the scene more than mere landscape beauty; for these little demesnes suggest ideas of humble comfort – peace – innocence – and all that is pleasing in rural associations. In many parts of England, where I happened to know the condition of the poor, I have looked at their lovely cottages, as one would at the corpse of a beauty. But in Monmouthshire all is cheerful. The cottages seem indeed poor, but not dependent. Each has his own cow – his little field – his garden – and for the most part, his orchard. Few of them therefore sink into paupers.

Monmouth is a very old town, clean, but shabby. It has been fortified, and one gate at least is still standing. The castle has almost disappeared. There is a very old bridge across the Wye, which is here a considerable stream, somewhat affected by the tide. From the top of a steep hill, which forms its bank on the side opposite the town, we had a view of a most splendid valley – varied by rising grounds – skirted by hills which are gay with every sort of cultivation – and terminated by the Welsh mountains at a distance of from fifteen to twenty miles. No scene of greater richness, variety and beauty have I seen in England. The whole is like Mosaic work; without one blank. There are no frightful squares, and straight lines in Monmouthshire fences. The colours too are much richer than those of a Scotch landscape. The wheat is a more golden yellow; the grass is unspeakably green; the very fallows are of a rich purpleish brown. The woods are natural, and therefore they are more feathery, and less formal than our plantations. Nothing could be added to the beauty of this country, if the mountains in the background were a little more imposing in their forms, and a little more proportioned in their height, to the plain from which they rise. But nothing less than the Alps would suit such a scene.

The wind being high, and blowing straight up the river, and the weather being showery, we abandoned all thoughts of sailing down the Wye. The post road to Chepstow is very bad; and for seven miles from Monmouth, nearly a continued climb; but the prospects are exquisite. The splendid country towards Abergavenny is almost constantly in sight, and the home views at every step present some new beauty. About nine miles from Monmouth we turned left into such a road!! "if road it can be called, which road was none". It threaded through wild closely wooded dells to Tintern . . . The celebrated abbey is nothing outside; but within, it is very fine, though not so fine as Fountains. Sketched the north-east corner. The road from thence to Piercefield is bad enough; not nearly so bad, however, as that we passed in the morning. Piercefield is really fine. There are two views which are exhibited under every possible aspect. The first is a noble reach of the Wye, winding round a meadow, which forms one of its banks, while the other rises into abrupt rocks and masses of wood. This bank is sometimes 150 feet high at least, while the other shelves in smooth green to the water's edge. The rocks are very noble; and though the river, even at high water, is too small for its magnificent accompaniments, yet, upon the whole, I have seen nothing of the kind so fine in England. The other view is towards the Severn, which is here two miles broad, and therefore a splendid object, though the banks are remarkable only for their richness. The town and castle of Chepstow are the most striking features in this landscape. The situation of Chepstow is beautiful.

Leaving "beautiful Monmouth" was sad enough, but it grieved Mary even more to watch the funeral of an infant, carried to its grave by girls dressed in white with only the father attending, and, after breakfast at The Angel, to pass a prison on the outskirts of Chepstow and see the prisoners walking in chains.

Herefordshire was pretty, full of orchards and hopfields, with the Abergavenny hills in the distance, but not as interesting as the country they had just left. Mr B noticed, after their return home, that any mention of Monmouth was guaranteed to bring a sparkle to Mary's eyes.

Hereford Cathedral seemed too like the ones already seen to merit more than a repetitive epithet from Mary – proof that the exhaustion of their itinerary was beginning to show. The sixteen miles to Ledbury seemed long, and they were thankful to arrive at that old town on the slopes of the Malvern hills with its view of the newly-built Eastnor Castle, where Lord Somers had in its grounds one of the twelve mistletoe oaks in England. Here, there was again a chance to relax before setting off for Worcester. Mary, feeling better, saw the town as of "a very handsome appearance; having several spires and towers, besides those of the fine cathedral". They stayed at the Hop-Pole Inn.

Another ten days of activity lay ahead before they returned to Edinburgh at the end of August. Predictably, Worcester could not be visited without seeing the making of porcelain. It gave Mary another opportunity for recording every detail:

> *Mr. F., a most polite and obliging person, called early, and introduced us at Chamberlayne's porcelain factory. Every part of the process was shewn to us. Flints are first calcined, which whitens them perfectly; then, mixed in certain proportions with grey Cornish granite, they are ground to so fine a powder as to pass through the closest silk. Water is poured upon this powder, and it is twice strained through silk sieves. The mixture is boiled till it is as thick as cream, and evaporated till it becomes a tough paste. Pieces of it are then placed upon a turning-wheel; and moulded, solely by hand, with wonderful precision and rapidity. This is the case, at least, with all the pieces of a circular form such as bowls, plates, cups and saucers. Dishes of other forms are made in gypsum moulds which, though they fit closely at first, soon absorb the moisture, so as to part very freely with the vessel which they have modelled. Every piece is then placed in a separate clay case. The furnace is filled with these; built closely up; and subjected to a red heat for sixty hours. It is then allowed to cool; the porcelain is withdrawn and in this state is called the biscuit. It is greatly diminished in size by this process. It is now ready to receive the blue colour which is cobalt, and looks of a dirty grey till exposed to the action of the glazing.*
>
> *The glazing consists of lead, and glass ground to an impalpable*

powder, mixed with certain secret ingredients in water. The biscuit is merely dipped into the glazing, and is then baked again for forty hours. It is now ready to receive all the other colours which the pattern may require, and the gilding. It is then baked a third time for ten hours or more, according to the colours employed. Lastly, the gilding is burnished with bloodstone or agate, and the china is ready for the wareroom. The colours are changed by baking. The greens, when laid on, are very imperfect; the rose colour is a dull purple; and the gilding is as black as ink. The painting-room had an unwholesome smell, and its inmates looked sickly. This manufacture is perfectly intelligible throughout, and therefore interesting. You can follow the flint and granite till, through seventeen different processes, they become a gilded tea-cup. From the china manufactory, we were carried to the cathedral. It is the finest, after York, which we have seen. Worcester is altogether a very pretty town, in a very fine situation. The streets are broad and clean, with good pavement. They wind a little, but not awkwardly. The shops are handsome. The chief trade is in gloves, which the women make at home. This must be better both for health and morals, than assembling them in large workshops.

The following day they were in Kidderminster – "a very ugly, mean-looking place, with no pavement in the streets". Tired after the big day in Worcester, Mary dismissed the carpet-making process quite briefly, "after the web is laid, the weaving is so entirely mechanical that children learn it in a week". As the tour progressed, a pattern emerged. Her enthusiasm for places that caught her emotions or fascinated her by their intricate productive processes, took so much out of her physically that her diary entries for what immediately followed were almost dull.

The show-place at Hagley, their next stop, was the Palladium Hall in its landscaped park, complete with rotunda, Ionic temple and Gothic ruins. This she quickly dismissed as "ugly, with a great superfluity of temples, seats, and objects of all sorts", and was annoyed that the peace of their inn was disturbed by the noise from the parties who were being taken round it. But, two days after Worcester, she was sufficiently rested to enjoy a Sunday visit to the village church in the grounds of Lord Lyttleton's estate which was attended by "a very decent-looking congregation", and to see in the church the monument to Sir Thomas Lucy who was said to have caught Shakespeare poaching on his land at Charlecote Manor.

Travelling on to Birmingham through Stourbridge and Hales Owen, they passed through a manufacturing village called Mud City which Mary described as inhabited by creatures whose savage habits had made them the terror of all those who were travelling in the area:

> *They owe their present half-civilisation to the charity of Mr Hill, a neighbouring squire, who has built and endowed a church, and has established a school among this horde of barbarians. He has a large family of his own, whom may God prosper!*

Birmingham was classified as "a vile hole" when Mary learnt that someone (whom she could only call "an animal"), was proposing to cut down the old oak trees at Hagley. Their plans to call on their friends Mr & Mrs James Watt were frustrated as they were away in Scotland. Greenock-born James had married his second wife after his move from Glasgow to Birmingham. In his working life at Glasgow University, he had made lifelong friendships characteristic of those whose moods of self-confidence are interspersed with moods of depression and self-doubt – a quality which attracted Mary to him. One of his friends was John Robinson, Professor of Natural Philosophy in Edinburgh, who once burst unannounced into James's house and found him sitting with a little "tin cistern" on his knee, working on it with his soldering iron heating in the fire. When asked how his experiment was going, James remarked brusquely, "You need not fash yourself any more about that, man; I have now made an engine that shall not waste a particle of steam. It shall all be boiling hot – ay, and hot water injected if I please". He then put the little cistern on the floor and gently kicked it out of sight under the table. Later Robinson learnt that this was the invention of the separate condenser.

Watt's partnership with Matthew Boulton when they launched the Boulton and Watt steam-engine business is legendary. The

Watts lived at Heathfield Hall, but the lovely surrounding parkland, with its glorious trees, flowering shrubs, waving grasses and a large pool with water-lilies – far from the chimneys and furnaces of Birmingham at Handsworth, is now all built over.

The Bruntons were very disappointed not to see James. Soon after they settled in Edinburgh he had come there as a guest of the Friday Club – the Edinburgh equivalent of the Lunar Society – of which he was a member. It met at the time of the full moon so that its members could have the benefit of its light when travelling home. On this occasion, another guest was Walter Scott, who described the impression that the ageing inventor made:

> *Amidst the company stood Mr. Watt, the man whose genius discovered the means of multiplying our national resources to a degree perhaps even beyond his own stupendous powers of calculation and combination, bringing the treasures of the abyss to the summit of the earth . . . Methinks I yet see and hear what I shall never see or her again . . . the alert, kind, benevolent old man had his attention alive to everyone's question, his information at everyone's command.*

Birmingham's "development" swallowed up Watt's home, Heathfield Hall, after his death, and the house was demolished. But James's workshop has been re-erected in the South Kensington Museum in London.

Another disappointment for the Bruntons was at not being able to see over Thomason's factory because a "wake" was taking place, so they filled in the time at the circulating library where Mary found, "on depositing the price, we were entrusted with four volumes of trash".

The next day being wet, they spent it at an exhibition of pictures which they decided must be "last year's outcasts from Somerset House", but in the afternoon at last there was the chance to inspect Thomason's manufactory, where button-eyes were made with an ingenious machine:

> *One part of it pushes forward the wire; a second bends it into a loop; a third cuts it; a fourth flattens the points that they may join the better with the button; a fifth pushes the eye when*

completed out of the machine. After all, the movement does not seem very complicated; if I would have had it myself for half an hour, I think I might have fully understood it. What makes me slow of comprehension when any one is bye? I believe it is because I am distracted by considering what the byestanders will think I am about.

This 1815 English tour did not lack variety. Next they went to see the Birmingham industry of silver-plating:

The plating on steel is executed after the article is perfectly formed. The iron knife, fork or spoon is dipped into a solution of sal-ammoniac, to cleanse it from grease. It is then powdered with resin to make the solder adhere to the steel, with which it has no affinity. Next it is dipped in the boiling solder; lead and tin. Then it is instantly fitted with a coat of pure silver, rolled out thin and perfectly flexible; this is pared round the edges with a knife. The article, whatever it is, is then passed through a heat strong enough to melt the solder without affecting the silver. The solder is squeezed out, and falls away in drops; the silver remains adhering perfectly to the steel. One side only of each article is plated at a time; the silver, by this means, overlaps the edges, and is double where it is most liable to waste. When the goods are finished, they are polished, first by a fine file, then by a leather wheel, and lastly by the human hand.

Leaving Birmingham, Mary found the country pretty, "so far as the smoke of 10,000 furnaces would allow us to see it". The Inn at Colebrook-dale was comfortable, giving them a rest before seeing the iron bridge over the Severn, built by Abraham Darby, whose wife, Deborah, had been their friend until her death in 1812. Abraham's discovery of how to smelt iron with coal instead of wood had given the world ample supplies of metal for making machines. His bridge, which Mary thought "beautifully light", was the first in the world to be made of iron, and was a symbol of the prosperity that iron was to bring to this remote and pastoral valley. The area along the banks of the Severn at Coalbrook was then throbbing with industry:

> *The first valley, which, however, is not the true Colebrook-dale, is really a strange-looking place. The steep and lofty banks of the Severn have been torn and disfigured in search of materials for manufacture, till they exhibit such appearances as might be supposed to follow an earthquake – fissures, cavities, mounds, heaps of broken stones, and hills of ashes and scoriae (fragments of cellular lava). The dell, which seems intended by nature for a quiet solitude, soothed by the hush of waters and the wooings of the cushet, resounds with the din of hammers, the crackling of flames, and the groanings of engines and bellows. All is shrouded in dense smoke; and on the few spots of vegetation which man has left undisturbed, the scanty foliage of the coppice is black, and the very weeds look scathed and unwholesome. Colebrook-dale, properly so called, runs in a different direction from this first valley; and resembles it only in harbouring one great iron-work. Colebrook is a very lovely valley still; and more so, for having been planted and adorned by Mr. Reynolds. He has led walks along its banks with great taste; and, with equal liberality, leaves them open to the public.*

Their next visit was to "Rose's china manufactory" where the delicate Coalport china was made:

> *It is upon a still larger scale than that at Worcester, but is carried on in the same manner. Here we saw many women employed in painting the china; but we were told that, though they serve the same apprenticeship as the men, under the same teacher, their work is always inferior. Here also we saw the printing of china; a process quite new to me. On copper-plate, properly engraved, the colour is laid, heated, and well rubbed in; a sheet of cambric paper, prepared with secret composition, is then printed from this plate. This paper is cut to fit the cup, saucer, etc., and pressed closely to fit it; the biscuit is then washed in cold water when the paper peels off, and the pattern remains perfectly impressed.*

The country towards Shrewsbury was pretty and Mary was surprised to see the Wrekin within a mile of the road. Once there, she admired the mall along the riverside, but the town seemed "a confused mass of ugly old houses; a labyrinth of lanes, as rugged as the paths of virtue, and as dirty and winding as those of vice". There were redeeming features in handsome houses at one end of the town, and in the elegant church of St Chad's. The rather uninteresting road to Oswestry was obscured by heavy rain, with only brief glimpses of the fine Montgomery hills. The entrance to North Wales lay ahead, and Mary's enthusiasm was soon in full spate again:

> *Chirk is a beautiful village, washed by a stream of the same name; the banks very steep, and the dell which they form is crossed by an aqueduct. A far finer aqueduct, fifteen arches, crosses the Dee as you enter the Vale of Llangollen. The Dee itself is a lively foaming stream, and looks more beautiful from being contrasted with the rivers of England. Near the town of Llangollen, its rich and populous valley is narrowed by the hill on which are the ruins of Dinas Bran. They make no great figure as you approach. The village very much resembles a Highland one: as unlike to an English village as possible! It is built in narrow shabby streets. The walls of the houses consist of thin grey stones – shewing the mortar beneath. The "Hand" is an old-fashioned house, but exceedingly comfortable.*

Under a burning August sun they climbed to see the ruins of the castle at Dinas Bran where they got a wide view of the valley surrounded by hills. Mary thought the view to the north was as desolate as any she had seen in Scotland:

> *We endeavoured, as usual to find the shortest way to Valle Crucis, and, as usual found only the worst. We passed a very Scotch-looking farmyard, where the children were bare-footed, and spoke Welch (sic). They all, however, can ask for a halfpenny in English.*

The ruins of Valle Crucis, are the most impressive monastic remains in North Wales. The Early English windows and the rose window can still be seen, and the 14th century sacristry and chapter house, with the dormitory on the first floor remain. Mary found this "pretty" – not grand, disappointed that the ruins were disfigured by farm offices. But compensation for this came when they spent an afternoon with the "Ladies of Llangollen", Eleanor Butler and Sarah Ponsonby, two eccentric recluses who had never left their home, Plas Newydd, for fifty years. They held court in this black and white house to important personalities, and the Bruntons found themselves included after attending a Sunday church service in Welsh.

On the last Monday of their holiday they travelled up the river Dee for breakfast at Corwen, the market town associated with Owen Glendower, the Welsh chieftain who, before his death in 1415, was a formidable opponent of King Henry IV of England. Mary loved this "beautiful, winding, lively and impetuous" river, but found the hills rather tame and the valley more wooded than most of those in the Highlands. Corwen emerges in her diary as "a bare, mean village, with nothing interesting except the blind harper – who has a first-rate natural genius. His execution is most wonderful – the difficulties of his instrument considered. His variations to his national airs are perfectly original and characteristic":

> *An Irish gentleman issued from a parlour on purpose to make the performer change his strain to the "washerwoman" and "Paddy O'Rafferty". But when he was called on for "King's Anthem", he fairly defeated his director by adding variations of such spirit and invention as gave the old air all the charm of novelty. Guessing that we might have our national partialities, he volunteered "Roslin Castle", and played it well; he assured me that an old woman had been his only teacher.*

As the journey neared its end, Mary's diary wound up with summaries and comparisons:

> *Wales may be inexhaustible to a landscape painter, with its endless rocks and ruins and hills, which he can exaggerate into something grand enough to fill the imagination. But give me the woody sheltered land where, at every turn, a spire, a smoke, the crowing of a cock, the shouting of a child, lead the fancy to half a dozen of irregular cottages, dropped upon a smooth little green,*

and peeping from among their own vines and roses! Oh England! the very sight of thy sweet hamlets mends the heart!

This second English holiday had sharpened her awareness of the influence on people of their environment. As they travelled homewards, her thoughts automatically turned to Scotland where, "though all is bare and naked, every thing bespeaks improvement, industry, intelligence; independence in the poor, and enterprize in the rich". She found the road to Edinburgh "right Scotch . . . bleak and dreary, but judicious and substantial".

I sigh over the thoughts of an Englishman's impressions on visiting mother Scotland, as Shem and Japhet did over their parent! No wonder if we be reflecting, frugal race! The gay images of spring and the luxuriance of summer never intrude on us, suggesting frolic and profusion! No wonder if we be hospitable, where one eternal winter constantly reminds us to draw together and be social.

Emmeline and the Later Years

The house at Albany Row near the centre of Edinburgh in a row of Georgian-style buildings, had much the same appearance then as it has today. But it has now merged with No. 37 to make premises for St. Mary's Roman Catholic Primary School at the corner of Albany Street and York Lane.

Mary found it hard to settle after their last holiday. The illness which Mr B had called an "aguish" complaint, recurred; she felt depressed, and her general health was poor. She wanted to start writing, but couldn't decide on a subject. A whole year passed before she wrote to Mrs Izett again:

> *I am as much in the open air as this melancholy summer has allowed me. As for my writing, it has been four months entirely discontinued. For the greater part of that time I have been utterly incapable of interesting myself in that, or indeed any other employment. The worst consequence, however, of my indisposition has been the uneasiness it has given to Mr B; to him especially, for he has felt it so much; and this has no doubt, tended to increase it. I trust that it is now removed and that I shall, when an endless train of visitors allows me, be able to take my talent from its napkin. Do not write to me either reproof or exhortation. I might have done something to rouse myself, but I had lost the will. I write without mood or coherence, for I do not aim at either. I am setting down my thoughts as they occur. Make out the feelings which prompt them as best you can . . . - There is a most overpowering Memoir of Cowper by himself. If you have not seen it, pray get it! You will be astonished by its power!*

She told William of her dilemma:

> *Writing is now become part of my duty. When I ask your advice, however, I openly make the reservation which most people, in the same case, make secretly – I will take your advice only if it please me. I am thinking of short tales; but have scarcely devised any subject for them. I do not need to write for bread; and I would not write one volume to gain the favour of Homer. A moral therefore is necessary for me; but where to get one on which to found a tale which will be readable is the question. A lofty moral, too, is necessary to my style of thinking and writing; and really it is not easy to make such a one the ground-work of any story which novel readers will endure. One advantage, indeed, I possess – the path which I have chosen is almost exclusively my own. The few moral lessons which our English fictions profess to teach are of the humblest class. Even Miss Edgworth's genius has stooped to inculcate mere worldly wisdom. "Patience is a plaster for all sores." – "Honesty is the best policy." – "A penny saved is a penny got", – seem the texts which she has embellished with her shrewd observation, and exquisite painting of character. To cut short this endless subject, some evening when you have nothing else to do, sit down, and let me hear your sentiments at great length. As I said before, I will adopt them if I like them.*

As they settled down for the winter, Mr B noticed how hesitant she was at the thought of starting another book, and suggested that she might write a series of essays on Cowper, but in the sixteen years since Cowper's death there had been many eulogies, and she didn't feel inclined to add to them. Eventually, she decided to keep to her original theme, but first wanted to please Mr B by writing a collection of short stories with the uninspiring title of *Domestic Tales*. The first, *The Runaway*, dealt with a truant boy whose experiences of hardship were to teach him the values of home. She tried to include a description of Orkney, but found it difficult to remember everything as clearly as she wished. So she returned to the old familiar ground.

Emmeline is her interpretation of the situation that arises when a divorced wife marries her seducer and does not find happiness.

The first chapter is headed by a quotation from John Newton, the clergyman friend of William Cowper.

As before, she aimed at making an instant impact by describing Emmeline's preparations for her "nuptial hour" – her wedding to Sir Sidney de Clifford, "a soldier of high fame . . ., a lover who adored her with all the energies of a powerful mind. She had youth and beauty and he was the husband of her choice whom she loved . . . yet the sigh which swelled her bosom was not the sigh of rapture – it was wrung from her by bitter recollections: for Emmeline had, before, been a bride".

Mr B suggested that, as with *Discipline*, she should make a synopsis, so she drew one up. Here are the essential ingredients of the unfaithful wife, the still-loving husband and the dissatisfied lover. The army background re-appears, but although traces of Mary's father can be detected in the military characters in *Self-Control* and *Discipline*, there is no question that he undergoes a reincarnation in the guise of De Clifford in *Emmeline*.

Part of Mary's difficulty with this third novel was her awareness of her limited experiences, and her effort not to be repetitive. She remembered hearing about her uncle Edward Ligonier challenging his wife's lover to a duel, and made De Clifford, insanely jealous of Devereux, do the same. But although Emmeline, by the time that Mary had reached Chapter V, was emerging from her trough of self-pity, and deciding to sublimate her problems by concerning herself with those of others, Mary's own spirits were low. Only with difficulty did she manage to cope with everyday visitors, and the demanding involvement of public charities. Early in her marriage she had resolved to investigate personally every case of parish hardship that came to her notice, and this involved her in intense preoccupation.

She hoped that after a summer break in the country she would get on better, but she had another feverish attack and felt even more depressed. One thing which cheered her was the invitation from a friend to hear extracts from Walter's Scott's *Guy Mannering* being read aloud at the time that it was going to press. This, because of her undying admiration for Scott, cheered her, and she could not wait to enthuse to William about Scott's next book:

December 1816

All Edinburgh was talking (till the Grand Duke Nicholas arrived to a change of the subject) of the volumes, which you must have seen advertised, under the titles "Tales of my Landlord". Beyond doubt they are from the same hand with Guy Mannering, though the author has changed his publisher for concealment. The four volumes contain two tales. The last, the longest, and by very far the best, is a story of the days of the Covenanters; in which, by and by, our ancestor Balfour of Burleigh makes a very scurvy figure. The conscientious and heroic, though often misguided, Covenanters are treated with little candour, and less mercy. But, notwithstanding all this, the tale is one of ten thousand. The description – the exquisite drawing of character – the humour – the unrivalled fertility of invention – or rather the boundless observation, which are shown in this Old Mortality, would immortalise the author even if he had no former claim to immortality. I cannot, however, allow that I think it equal, upon the whole, to Guy Mannering.

But the enthusiasm was only temporary. The sudden death of a young friend affected her deeply. Trying to rid herself of introspection, she tried to master Gaelic again. Mr B suggested that she might study Latin and Greek, but she felt it was too big a subject for her to tackle. William's wife was teaching classics to their daughter, Mary Henrietta, which gave Mary the opportunity to write her views about women and languages to her sister-in-law:

I am glad that you are teaching Mary Latin. It seems to me, that nature itself points out the propriety of teaching women languages, by the facility with which we generally acquire them. I never knew a girl, who, in learning the dead languages, did not keep above the boys in her class; nor did I ever happen to see this acquisition produce a female pedant. Indeed, learning of all kinds is now too common among ladies, to be any longer like Cain's mark, excluding the bearer from all human intercourse. I know a lady who, two years ago, gained a mathematical prize, from Oxford I think, with perfect impunity, being still universally received as a very agreeable womanly sort of person.

> *I am clearly for furnishing women with such accomplishments as are absolutely incapable of being converted into a matter of exhibition; and such, in the present state of society, are classical learning and mathematics. These hard times compel so many women to celibacy that I should think it no bad speculation to educate a few for respectable old maids; especially such as have minds strong enough to stand alone, and romantic enough not to choose to marry merely for the sake of being married. Luckily, the education which fits a woman for leading apes with a good grace, will not spoil her for suckling fools, and chronicling small beer. Whether your Mary is to marry or not, I hope she will grow up with a mind vigorous and happy in its own resources, trained as a mind ought to be, which is soon to shake off its connection with all material objects, and to owe its sole happiness to improvement in knowledge and goodness. As for boys, the world will educate them in spite of you. You may "plant and water", but the rude blast will soon give your sprouts their own direction; nor can they, like our happier sex, hide themselves from its influence. Reading, reflection, and advice, do much to form the character of women. Men are creatures of circumstances and of example; half a dozen witty profligates will put to flight a dozen years' maxims in an afternoon. But as the old saying has it, "They are well kept whom God keeps; and some are wonderfully kept – some as wonderfully restored". By this time, I fancy you think I am borrowing a page from the Doctor's incipient volume.*

Mr B, after being awarded the honour of wearing the black and purple hood of a Doctor of Divinity of Edinburgh University, began preparing fifteen sermons and lectures for publication.

In the spring of 1818, at the age of 39, Mary found that she was pregnant. *Emmeline* came to a standstill as the symptoms of approaching motherhood made themselves felt. But by the summer she was feeling quite well again and Mr B offered up prayers of thankfulness, convinced that the coming of their child would restore her to full health. But in spite of her renewed strength, Mary was convinced that her confinement would prove fatal. Try as he could, Mr B found himself powerless to influence her against it. At 46 years of age, excited at the thought of becoming a father for the first time, he had to cope, not with the excitements that normally precede a baby's arrival, but with a wife who was making preparations for her death, choosing the clothes that she wished to be buried in, selecting and labelling tokens of remembrance for her closest friends, and arranging for obituary notices to be sent out in her own handwriting. To his astonishment, this was carried out with quiet determination and no diminution of her usual cheerfulness. It was as if she was preparing to meet death, or a return to her usual robust health, on equal terms. The last thing she wanted to do was to distress her friends with her premonition, so she continued to immerse herself in welfare work and concern for others.

There is a mixture of fortitude and tenderness in her last letter to William's wife:

> *October 22 1818*
>
> *If it please God Almighty to spare my infant's life and my own, I trust I am "made of sterner stuff" than to shrink from a few hours of pain which nature can support. I suppose the trial will be made about three weeks hence. I hope not sooner; for even then I shall scarcely be ready. Ready! do I say? What time would be necessary to prepare me for the change which I must probably then undergo! But there is ONE with whom one day is a thousand years! When I spoke of preparation, I merely meant that I had not "set my house in order"... May God bless dear William, and you, in your family, and in all your concerns; but chiefly in that great concern of making your conduct in this life a preparation for a better! I shall not write again. My husband will.*

Her anticipation, in the end, proved correct. After giving birth to a stillborn son on 7 December 1818, three weeks later than expected, she recovered for a few days with a rapidity which surprised her doctors, but had another sudden fever and died on the morning of Saturday, 19 December 1818, at 35 Albany Street, just seven weeks after her 40th birthday.

Nine days later, the *Edinburgh Evening Courant* published a long and appreciative obituary, a panegyric of both Mary and her work.

On 29 December, the *Edinburgh Advertiser* published its own tribute, dwelling on her spirit of Christianity, humble piety, active benevolence and personal purity, stressing her superintendence of The Institute for the Poor every day, and her extensive private charity and many unseen good deeds. In reporting that she had undertaken to teach "the highest lessons of religion and virtue in fiction", the writer quoted Mary as saying, "There is high authority for using fable as the vehicle of important, even of solemn truth", and described her as never having had the vanity of authorship.

Joanna Baillie was shocked and saddened by Mary's death. Shortly before the publication of *Self-Control*, her new play *The Family Legend* was performed in Edinburgh with a prologue by Walter Scott, but whether Mary went to see it we do not know. Joanna wrote a 47-line obituary poem as a sincere tribute from one celebrated 19th-century Scottish authoress to another who had become her friend.

Mary's many other friends felt that a fuller account of her literary life and her success as a writer would provide the public, and posterity, with an insight into how she composed her novels. Mr B was asked if he would write a Memoir. He hesitated to accept while his grief was still new, but later felt grateful for a task with a definite purpose to undertake on behalf of his wife. It began:

> *It has been for twenty years my happiness to watch the workings of that noble mind – my chief usefulness to aid its progress, however feebly. Nothing is more soothing to me now than to dwell on the remembrance of her – nothing more dear than to diffuse the benefit of her example. I know that I shall perform the task very inadequately. Were I better qualified than I am for its discharge, the relation which I bore to her makes it needful for me to repress feelings upon which any other biographer would have dwelt with delight. But if I can make her memory useful to one of her fellow-creatures, this is the only consideration that her sainted spirit would prize.*

He finished the memoir on 2 March 1819, and persuaded Mary's publishers to issue the five chapters of the unfinished *Emmeline* with it, including extracts from her letters. It was published as "*Emmeline*, with some other pieces by Mary Brunton, author of

Self-Control and *Discipline,* to which is prefixed a Memoir of her life, including some extracts from her correspondence". Mr B inscribed the book, "affectionally and respectfully" to Captain William Balfour, R.N., and added his own message of farewell:

Vale!
Heu quanto minus est
Cum reliquis versari
quam tui
meminisse!

Mr B selected extracts from her diaries of the English holidays which he thought would illustrate her love of landscape scenery, her emotional appreciation of devotional works of art, and her meticulous investigation of subjects which might have appeared the least likely to attract a woman. Very few passages refer to their life together. No family secrets are given away, no hint of the depths of the problems with his mother-in-law, nothing which might induce unwelcome publicity.

He did not find the composing of it easy:

Of her literary character, I have endeavoured to give a true, though feeble outline. They who have merely heard of her as the author of two once popular novels, if they ever glance at these pages at all, may think I have said too much. But I am sure the detail will not seem tedious to those who met her in the intercourse of private life; or who examined her books with care enough to estimate from them what the author might have been capable of performing…

…I am persuaded, that in all which she had done she was only trying her strength; and that if her life had been prolonged, the standard of female intellect might have been heightened, and the character of English literature might have been embellished by her labours…

He was on more familiar ground when he came to the subject of Mary's devotion to Christianity. It is very long, very detailed and very comprehensive, and only a part of it is quoted here:

... She had the highest reverence for the Common Prayer Book of the Church of Scotland, and her guide in the duty of self-examination was Bishop Gibson's little book upon the Lord's Supper. She was too deeply convinced of the importance of self-examination not to be regular and strict in discharging it. She recorded in writing, at least twice in every year, the answers which her conscience enabled her to give to the different topics of enquiry which are suggested by Bishop Gibson, and on comparing this record from time to time she wrote down the inferences by which she desired that her conduct might be guided. The only direct contribution which she has left to the spiritual welfare of her fellow-creatures beyond what is contained in her works already published, is the fragment inserted in this volume, under the title which she herself has given it, of HELPS TO DEVOTION. It is published in exactly the state in which she left it. Some one, I trust, of judgment as sound, of affections as warm, and of piety as ardent as her own, will complete the selection which she has begun ...

On one of the last occasions when I expressed to her my delight and gratitude for the increasing hopes of her recovery, her answer was; that though she could not but wish to live while her life was so valued, her earnest prayer had been that, in this and in every thing else, instead of her being allowed to choose for herself, her heavenly Father might do what was best for us both. Within two short days thereafter, the violence of fever suspended the expression of her feelings! God only knows with what bitterness of heart I longed that one ray of intelligence might return ere her departure; that I might hear her speak once again of her faith and hope; and that I might once again receive her blessing.

In the years following, Mr B immersed himself in the kind of literary work which she had encouraged him to undertake. *His Sermons and Lectures* were published in Edinburgh in the year of her death, and his main work, *Outlines of Persian Grammar with Extracts*, published in Edinburgh in 1822, became an acknowledged textbook. His crowning accolade came when he was appointed Moderator of the General Assembly of the Church of Scotland, taking up office on 22 May 1823.

After his year as Moderator, he was unanimously elected Convenor of the Church of Scotland's Commission on India Missions, an office which he held for 13 years. At the age of 65 he took on the Honorary Librarianship of Eden College which was devoted to the advancement of Science and Literature, at a salary of £30 a year with rented accommodation of £40. At 75, when staying with his niece, Anne Stevenson, at Bilstonbrae, Loanhead, Edinburgh, he was advised by his doctors in August 1847, to relinquish his Chair at the University, which he had held for 34 years. Unwilling to accept inactivity, he wrote to the Lord Advocate, asking to be considered for "a little office at the Chapel Royal" which had become vacant on the death of Dr Chalmers, but there is no record of his success in this application.

His service to the clerical and academic life of Edinburgh was acknowledged in 1846 when his portrait was painted by Sir John Watson Gordon, who painted prominent members of society, soldiers, sailors, survivors of the Napoleonic Wars, governors and administrators of colonies, Provosts, important figures in the Law, and in the Church, etc. This portrait hangs in the Talbot Rice Department of Edinburgh University.

With the onset of old age, and the lack of an heir, Mr B decided to dispose of most of his library, and in March 1848, instructed Tait & Nisbet, of 11 Hanover Street, Edinburgh ,to sell 2,211 of his books. In this year his last published work appeared, *Forms of Public Worship* in the Church of Scotland.

When his niece decided to move from Loanhead to keep house for her brother Patrick Stevenson, the minister at Coupar Angus, Mr B saw it as an opportunity to continue his association with the ministry, and moved with her. They settled at Jordanstone House, Meigle, Perthshire, where he was sometimes called on to officiate at public ceremonies, and sometimes in demand for composing fine inscriptions for foundation stones and memorial tablets either in dead or existing languages. One example of his expertise is the mural tablet erected by the Governors of Heriot's Hospital in memory of their treasurer, Mr Denham, who died in 1822.

Mr B died at Jordanstone House in his 82nd year – the 57th year of his ministry – on 9 February 1854. His will was witnessed by the gardener, and by Rev Alexander Duff, D.D., the first missionary to be sent to India by the Church of Scotland. The years that Mr B had spent as Convenor of the Commission on India Missions had cemented his friendship with Rev. Duff. But any hopes of discovering the whereabouts of the manuscripts of the Mary Brunton novels from scrutiny of this will were destined for disappointment. All that Mr B had to leave, with no mention of any manuscripts, was bequeathed to his niece, Anne Stevenson, "whom failing, to her brother, Rev. Patrick James Stevenson, minister of Coupar, and their respective heirs".

Many love stories are more sensationally romantic than that of Mary Balfour and Alexander Brunton, but few, if any, have the unlikely, yet extraordinarily appealing ingredients of the young girl from the Orkney Islands who rejected, regardless of strong parental pressure, a future that might have led to a dazzling London society marriage, in order to elope with the man of her choice who, in terms of worldly goods, had little to offer to his bride. But in his estimation, as in hers, worldly goods were of small importance, and played no part in the contribution that they each made to the age in which they lived. The poignancy of Mary's death at the height of her success has left behind a legacy of devotion, humility, a genius for friendship and an infectious joy in living which emerges in a piece that she wrote:

> *I believe nobody was ever better formed for enjoying life than I, saving and excepting in the construction of an abominable stomach, for I delight in travelling, yet can be happy at home; I enjoy company, yet I prefer retirement. I can look with rapture on the glorious features of nature – the dark lake and the rugged mountains – the roaring cataract – yet can gaze with no small pleasure on the contents of a haberdasher's window.*

When she and Mr B attended the funeral service for her uncle, David Balfour, in the spring of 1813, and the committal in the Canongate Kirkyard in Edinburgh, they decided that they too would rest there when their time came. It was nothing to do with the fact that the Canongate Kirkyard was the resting place of many famous Edinburgh contemporaries, such as Adam Smith, but it was the place where Mary could remain close to someone who was a link with her father, and Orkney, and her earliest involvement with Mr B. A modest plaque commemorates them on the west wall of the cemetery near to its north end, placed above the one to David Balfour and his wife Marion, and intimating that Mary and Mr B are buried nearby. It is only with difficulty that the inscription can be read:

> *In memory of the Reverend Alexander Brunton, D.D., one of the ministers of the Tron Church, Professor of Oriental Languages in the College of Edinburgh, born 2nd October 1772, died 9th February 1854. Also of Mary Brunton, his wife, authoress of Self-Control and other works, born 1st November 1778, died 19th December 1818.*

Synopsis of *Discipline* – Chapters X - XXII

The only part that seems to remain of Mary's outline of *Discipline* shows that she used the method of placing the number of each chapter at the head of a page in a very small book. Asterisks were used to mark the blank spaces which it was her intention to fill in as the story progressed. She made the outline to please Mr B, who had suggested it, but she seems to have added scarcely anything to the first draft. As with Self-Control, the narrative was allowed to develop in the finished manuscript, a method that she had found successful the first time.

*Chap. x. - Miss Mortimer's departure. - *Hackney-coach. - *Mr Maitland's eloquence. - Miss Mortimer's letter.*

*Chap. xi. - Ellen's reflections on Miss M's letter. - *Tries to make Mr Maitland jealous of Lord F, at Miss A's instigation.*

*Chap. xii. - Mr Maitland leaves her. - *Entanglement. - *Her father forbids. - *Ellen angry. - *Quarrels with Lady Maria about precedence. - These determine her. Such the amiable passions which sometimes instigate a love-match!*

Chap. xiii. - Elopement.

Chap. xiv. - Return.

*Chap. xv. - Application to Miss Arnold, and answer. - *Creditors offer her a small sum to subsist on for the present. - She disdainfully refuses. *Retires to -. *Alone, in want and desolate. - *Miss M comes. - Urges Ellen to go home with her. - Ellen suddenly drives* *her away. - Fido left behind. - Ellen weeps over him.*

CHAP. XVI. - *Goes home with Miss M. - *Shown room. - Bible. - *True repentance. - *Miss M's life and manners. - *Ellen, charmed with the eloquence of a Sectary, is going to join. - Miss M persuades her to pause.*

CHAP. XVII. - *Letter from Mr Maitland. - Story. - *Pays Lord F. - Meets Lady Maria. - Sells ring for Miss Mortimer. - *Miss M dies. - Ellen gives all to the old servant. *Contrast of E's sorrow with her former rebellious despair.*

CHAP. XVIII. - *Ellen, still proud, unwilling to enter into a menial life among acquaintances. - *Gets a letter of recommendation from Miss M's friend and goes to -. *Finds the lady absent. - Seeks a situation. - Engaged by a cunning fool. - *Mistress jealous that E has something concealed. - *Then jealous of her lover.*

CHAP. XIX. - *Mistress marries, and is quite engaged with her husband for the present. - *Always showing signs of jealousy. - *Ellen. - Fever. - Removed by mistress to a mad-house. - Blank in her recollections.*

CHAP. XX. - *Ellen's first recollections.*

CHAP. XXI. - *Ellen dismissed. - Sends for her clothes. - Sells some for subsistence. - Her delight in the fresh fields, etc. - *Meets Miss Arnold, a beggar. - Sells shawl. - Miss A sick - impatient - wretched. - Tells her story cunningly. - Retains the traits of cunning still; and of sly flattery, even where she has nothing to gain by it. - *Ellen, after many struggles, resolves to beg for her.*

CHAP. XXII. - *Sees her name in a newspaper advertisement. - *Journey. - Highland Inn. - Children. - Fowls. - Petticoat-bellows. - Tub-chimney. - Horse with creels. - *Scenery. - Glen Eredine. - *Castle Eredine. - Multitude of servants. - Old Chief. - Furniture. - Miss Graham's apartments. *Cecil sick. - broken-hearted for death of Mr Kenneth. - Visit to Cecil. - Cecil's song. - *Lord St. E.*

Selected Passages from *Self Control*

Lady Harriet has died. Captain Montreville is ill and poverty-stricken, unable to understand why Laura will not solve their financial problems by marrying the wealthy and handsome Colonel Hargrave who seems to adore her. He is ignorant of the fact that Hargraves once tried to seduce Laura and, even though she loves him, she has banished him for a period of two years in the hopes that he will reform. Anxious to help her father by earning some money she tries to sell her drawings, and, in desperation, decides to try for a post as a paid companion.

Laura knew that one of the most elegant houses in Grosvenor Street was inhabited by a Lady Pelham, the daughter of Lady Harriet Montreville's mother by a former marriage. She knew that, for many years, little intercourses had subsisted between the sisters; and that her father was even wholly unknown to Lady Pelham. But she was ignorant, that the imprudence of her mother's marriage served as the cause for a coldness, which had really existed before it had any such pretext.

With all her Scottish prejudice in favour of the claims of kindred (and Laura in this and many other respects was entirely a Scotch woman), she could not, without the utmost repugnance, think of applying to her relation. To introduce herself to a stranger whom she had never seen – to appear not only as an inferior, but as a supplicant – a beggar! Laura had long and successfully combated the innate pride of human nature; but her humility almost failed under this trial. Her illustrious ancestry – the dignity of a gentlewoman – to independence of one who can bear to labour and endure to want, all rose successively to her mind; for pride can wear many specious forms. But she had nearer claims than the honour of her ancestry – dearer concerns that her personal importance; and when she thought of her father, she felt that she was no longer independent.

Severe was her struggle, and bitter were the tears which she shed over the conviction that it was right that she should become a petitioner for the bounty of a stranger. In vain did she repeat to herself that she was a debtor to the care of Providence for her daily bread, and was not entitled to choose the means by which it was supplied. She could not conquer her reluctance. But she could act right in defiance of it. She could sacrifice her own feelings to the comfort of her father – to a sense of duty. Nay, upon reflection, she could rejoice that circumstances compelled her to quell that proud spirit with which, as a Christian, she maintained a constant and vigorous combat.

While these thoughts were passing in her mind, she had finished her drawing; and, impatient to know how far this sort of labour was likely to be profitable, she furnished her father with a book to amuse him in her absence; and, for the first time since they had occupied their present lodgings, expressed a wish to take a walk for amusement. Had Montreville observed the blushes that accompanied this little subterfuge, he would certainly have suspected that the amusement which this walk promised was of no common kind; but he was in one of his reveries, hanging over the mantle-piece, with his forehead resting on his arm, and did not even look up while he desired her not to be long absent.

She resolved to go first to Lady Pelham, that coming early she might find her disengaged, and afterwards to proceed to the print-shop.

The wind blew keen across the snow as Laura began her reluctant pilgrimage. Her summer attire, to which her finances could afford no addition, ill defended her from the blast. Through the streets of London she was to explore her way unattended. Accustomed to find both beauty and pleasure in the solitude of her walks, she was to mix in the throngs of a rude rabble, without protection from insult. But no outward circumstances could add to the feelings of comfortless dismay with which she looked forward to the moment when, ushered through stately apartments into the presence of self-important greatness, she could announce herself a beggar. Her courage failed – she paused, and made one step back towards her home. But she recalled her former thoughts. "I have need to be humbled", said she; and again proceeded on her way.

As she left the little garden that surrounded her lodgings, she perceived an old man who had taken shelter by one of the pillars of the gate. He shivered in the cold, which found easy entrance through the rags that covered him, and famine glared from his hollow eye. His grey hair streamed on the wind as he held out the tattered remains of a hat and said, "Please to help me, Lady. – I am very poor". He spoke in the dialect of her native land, and the accents went to Laura's heart; – for Laura was in the land of strangers. She had never been deaf to the petitions of the poor, for all the poor of Glenalbert were known to her; and she knew that what she spared from her own comforts was not made the minister of vice. Her purse was already in her hand, here she remembered that to give was become a crime.

As the thought crossed her, she started like one who had escaped from sudden danger. "No, I must not give you money", said she, and returned the purse into her pocket. "I am cold and hungry", said the man still pleading, and taking encouragement from Laura's relenting eye. "Hungry!" repeated Laura, "then come with me, and I will give you bread;" and she returned to the house to bestow on the old man the humble fare which she had before destined to supply her own wants for the day, glad to purchase by a longer fast the right to feed the hungry.

"In what respect am I better than this poor creature", said she to herself, as she returned with the beggar to the gate, "that I should offer to him with ease, and even with pleasure, what I myself cannot ask without pain. Surely I do not rightly believe that we are of the same dust! The same frail, sinful, perishable dust!"

But it was in vain that Laura continued to argue with herself. In this instance she could only do her duty; she could not love it. Her heart filled, and the tears rose to her eyes. She dashed them away – but they rose again.

When she found herself in Grosvenor Street, she paused for a moment. "What if Lady Pelham should deny my request? Dismiss me as a bold intruder? Why, then", said Laura, raising her head, and again advancing with a firmer step, "I shall owe no obligation to a stranger".

She approached the house and ascended the steps. Almost breathless she laid her hand upon the knocker. At that moment she imagined her entrance through files of insolent domestics into a room filled with gay company. She anticipated the inquisitive glances – shrunk in fancy from the supercilious examination; and she again drew back her hand. "I shall never have courage to face all this", thought she. While we hesitate, a trifle turns the scale. Laura perceived that she had drawn the attention of a young man on the pavement, who stood gazing on her with familiar curiosity; and she knocked, almost before she was sensible that she intended it.

The time appeared immeasurable till the door was opened by a maid-servant. "Is Lady Pelham at home?" inquired Laura, taking encouragement from the sight of one of her own sex. "No Ma'am", answered the maid, "my lady is gone to keep Christmas in —shire, and will not return for a fortnight". Laura drew a long breath, as if a weight had been lifted from her breast; and, suppressing an ejaculation of "thank Heaven", sprung in the lightness of her heart at one skip from the door to the pavement.

Selected Passages from *Discipline*

An only child, Ellen Percy, idolised, spoilt, and indulged by her parents to such an extent that she became self-willed, stubborn and almost uncontrollable, suffered a shock at the unexpected death of her mother and became even more impossible. Her father, "a man of business", who had started life with "'very slender advantages", had arrived at his present state of affluence by his own skill and diligence. Overcome with grief, and unable to cope single-handed with his daughter's tantrums, he sent her to a fashionable boarding-school where she stayed until she was in her sixteenth year. Ellen is the narrator throughout the novel:

At the Christmas holidays I quitted school, impatient to enter on the delights of womanhood. My father, whose ideas of relaxation were all associated with his villa at Richmond, determined that I should there spend the time which intervened before the commencement of the gay winter. In compliance with my request, he invited Miss Arnold, whose liberation took place at the same time with my own, to spend a few weeks with me – an invitation which was gladly accepted.

This indulgence, however, was somewhat balanced by the presence of a very different companion. My mother was a woman of real piety; and to her was accorded that 'medicine of life', which respectable authority has assigned exclusively to people of that character. She had a 'faithful friend'. This friend still survived, and in her my father sought a kind and judicious adviser for my inexperience. He pressed her to his house her permanent abode, and to share with him in the government of my turbulent spirit, until it should be consigned to her authority. Miss Elizabeth Mortimer, therefore, though she refused to relinquish entirely the independence of a home, left her cottage for a while to the care of her only maid-servant; and rejoicing in an occasion of manifesting affection for her departed friend, and pleasing herself with the idea that one bond of sympathy yet remained between them, prepared to revive her friendship to the mother in acts of kindness to the child.

I regret to say that she was received with sentiments much less amicable. Miss Arnold and I considered her a spy upon our actions, and a restraint upon our pleasures. We called her Argus and duenna; voted her a stick, a bore, a quiz, or, to sum up all reproach in one comprehensive epithet, a Methodist. Not that she really was a sectary. On the contrary, she was an affectionate and dutiful daughter of the establishment, countenancing schismatics no further than by adopting such of their doctrines and practices as are plainly scriptural, and by testifying towards them on all occasions, whether of opposition of conformity, a charity which evinced the divinity of its own origin. But Miss Mortimer displayed a practical conviction, that grey hairs ought to be covered with a cap, and that a neck of five-and-forty is the better for a handkerchief; she attended church regularly; was seldom seen in a public place; and above all, was said to have the preposterous custom of joining her own servants in daily prayer. Miss Arnold and I were persuaded that our duenna would attempt to import this 'pernicious superstition' into her new residence, and we resolved upon a vigorous resistance of her authority.

Our spirit, however, was not put to the proof. Miss Mortimer affected no authority. She seemed indeed anxious to be useful, but afraid to be officious. She was even so sparing of direct advice that, had she not been the most humble of human beings, I should have said that she trusted to the dignity and grace of her general sentiments, and the beautiful consistency of her example for affecting the enormous transition from what I was, to what I ought to be.

Her gentleness converted the dislike of her charges into feelings somewhat less hostile. My friend and I could find nothing offensive in her singularities; we therefore attempted to make them amusing.

We invented dismal cases of calamity, and indited piteous appeals to her charity, making her often trudge miles over the snow in search of fictitious objects of compassion; that we might laugh at the credulity which was never deaf to the cry of want, and at the principle which refused to give without enquiry. We hid her prayer-book; purloined her hoards of baby linen and worsted stockings; and pasted caricatures on the inside of her pew in church.

Much of the zest of these excellent jokes was destroyed by the calm temper and perverse simplicity of Miss Mortimer. If by chance she was betrayed into situations really ludicrous, nobody laughed with more hearty relish than she. Even on the more annoying of these practical jests, she smiled with good-natured contempt; never, even by the slightest glance, directing to Miss Arnold or myself the pity which she expressed for the folly of the contriver. We could never perceive that she suspected us of being her persecutors; and her simplicity, whether real of affected, compelled us to a caution and respect which we would have renounced had we been openly detected. Our jokes, however, such as they were, we carried on with no small industry and perseverance; every day producing some invention more remarkable for mischief than for wit. At last the tragic issue of one of our frolics inclined me to a suspension of hostilities; and had it not been for the superior firmness of my friend Miss Arnold, I believe I should have finally laid down my arms.

We were invited one day to dine with a neighbouring gentleman, a widower, whose family of dissipated boys and giddy girls were the chosen associates of Miss Arnold and myself. My father was otherwise engaged, and could not go; but Miss Mortimer accepted the invitation, very little to the satisfaction of the junior members of the party, who had projected a plan for the evening, with which her presence was likely to interfere. Miss Arnold and I, therefore, exerted all our ingenuity to keep her at home. We spilt a dish of tea upon her best silk gown; we pressed her to eat pineapple in hopes of exasperating her toothache; and we related to her a horrible robbery and murder which had been committed only the night before in the very lane through which we were to pass. These and many other contrivances proved ineffectual. As Miss Mortimer could not wear her best gown, she could go in a worse; she would not eat pineapple; and she insisted that those who had committed the murder only the night before must be bloody-minded indeed if they were ready to commit another. Next, I bribed the coachman to say that the barouche could not stir until it was repaired; but my father, who, on this occasion, seemed as determined as Miss Mortimer, insisting that we should go under her auspices or not go at all, settled that Miss Arnold should ride, while I drove Miss Mortimer in the curricle.

Highly displeased with this decision, I resolved that Miss Mortimer, whose forte certainly was not strength of nerve, should rue the mettle of her charioteer. With this good-natured purpose, I privately arranged that a race should be run between my steeds, and those which were mounted by Miss Arnold, and one of the fry which had already begun to swarm round the rich Miss Percy. We set off quietly enough, but we were no sooner out of sight of my father's windows, than the signal was given, and away we flew with the speed of lightening. I saw poor Miss Mortimer look aghast, though she betrayed no other sign of fear, and I had a malicious triumph in the thoughts of compelling her to sue for quarter.

'Is it not better, my dear', said she at last, 'to drive a little more deliberately? The road is narrow here, and if we were to run over some poor creature, I know you would never forgive yourself'.

There was such irresistable mildness in the manner of this expostulation that I could not disregard it; and I was checking my horses at the moment, when my beau, who had fallen behind, suddenly passed me. He gave them a triumphant smack with his whip, and the high-mettled animals sprang forward with a vigour that baffled my opposition. At this moment a decent-looking woman, in standing aside to let me pass, unfortunately threw herself into the line of his course, and I felt the horror which I deserved to feel, when my companions, each bounding over her, left her lying senseless within a step of the destruction which I had lost the power to avert.

From the guilt of murder I was saved by the fortitude of a stranger. He boldly seized the rein; and, with British strength of arm turning the horses short round, they reared, backed, and in an instant overturned the carriage. The stranger, alarmed by this consequence of his interference, hastened to extricate Miss Mortimer and myself;

while our jockeys, too intent on the race to look back, were already out of sight.

Miss Mortimer looked pale as death, and trembled exceedingly; yet the moment she was at liberty she flew to the poor woman, whom the stranger raised from the ground. They chafed her temples, and administered every little remedy which they could command, while I stood gazing on her in active alarm. At length she opened her eyes; and so heavy a weight was lifted from my heart, that I could not refrain from bursting into tears; but unwilling to exhibit these marks of a reproving conscience, I turned proudly away.

Bibliography

CHAPTER I

The Complete Peerage, Revised Edition of 1929, St Catherine's Press.

The Army Lists 1775-1798, National Library of Scotland.

Field-Marshal Ligonier - Story of the British Army, Rex Whitworth, Oxford Clarendon Press, 1958.

The Universal Scots Almanac, 1769.

Debrett's Guide to Tracing Your Ancestry, Noel Currer-Briggs and Royston Gambier. Webb & Bower, 1984.

Annals of Gallantry 1814-15, A. Moore.

Autobiography of Vittorio Amadeus Alfieri, 1749-1803.

D'Alton's Army Lists, Vol. V, Part II, Page 46.

George II, Vol. II, Page 140. Horace Walpole.

Ordnance Gazetteer for Scotland. Groome, Vol. III, Page 4, McKenzie, Edinburgh & Glasgow.

CHAPTER II

History of Orkney. W.P.L. Thomson, The Mercat Press, Edinburgh, 1987.

The Balfours and Balfour Castle. Mary Zawadzki and Dr R.P. Fereday.

Mr David Bryce. Valerie Fiddes & Alistair Rowan, University of Edinburgh, 1976.

The Men Who Ruled India. Philip Woodruff, Jonathan Cape, 1952.

Noltland Castle. W. Douglas Simpson, C.B.E., M.A., D.Litt., F.S.A., F.S.A.(Scot.), Hon. F.R.I.A.S.

The Orkney Library Archive Room, Kirkwall, Orkney.

Thomas Balfour. Irene Rosie, Kirkwall Grammar School, 1978.

The Northern Isles, Orkney and Shetland. Alexander Fenton, John Donald, Edinburgh, 1978.

CHAPTER III

The Orkney Library Archive Room, Kirkwall, Orkney.

The Ordnance Survey Original Name Books, Survey of 1877-78.

Orkney. Patrick Bailey, David & Charles, 1971, Reprint 1974.

Inventory of the Bu of Burray. Patrick Fea of Airy, 1747.
Ordnance Gazetteer of Scotland. Groome. Wm. McKenzie, Edinburgh & Glasgow.
H.M.S.O. Scotland.
The Orkney Sasines, 1781-1860. New Register House, Edinburgh.
The Story of the House of Graemeshall in Orkney. Pateas Amicis, Patrick Sutherland Graeme, Kirkwall, 1936.

CHAPTER IV

Education in Edinburgh in the 18th Century. Alexander Law, University of London Press, 1965.
Scott's Fasti. Synod of Lothian & Tweeddale, page 137.
The Balfours and Balfour Castle. Mrs L. Balfour-Kinnear. Edited M. Zawadzki.
Topographical Dictionary of Scotland, Vol. I, 1813.
New Statistical Account of Bolton, 1836, Revised 1838.
The Parish Church of Bolton. Information Sheet. Rev. George Loudon.
Alexander Brunton's Memoir of the Life and Writings of his wife with extracts from her correspondence, 1819, printed with the unfinished *Emmeline* by Manners & Miller, 1819.
The Old Hearse of Bolton. E.J. Wilson. Scrapbook Vol. 35. Adam Scott, 1898, Haddington Library, East Lothian.
Session Minutes of Bolton Church. Haddington Library.
Sketches of the Edinburgh Clergy of the Established Church of Scotland. John Anderson, 1832.
East Lothian. Charles E. Green. William Green & Sons, Edinburgh & London, 1907.
Edinburgh in the Nineteenth Century, 1800-1900. Edited W.M. Gilbert, published J. & R. Allan Ltd., 80-86 South Bridge, Edinburgh, 1901.
History of Orkney. W.P.L. Thomson. The Mercat Press, Edinburgh, 1987.
Register of Marriages in the City of Edinburgh 1751-1800. F.H. Grant, W.S., 1922.
The Orkney Library Archive Room, Kirkwall, Orkney.
The Bolton Hearse and Graveguard. J. Norman Cartwright, F.S.A. Scot.

CHAPTER V

The Galleys at Lepanto. Jack Beeching. Charles Scribener & Sons, New York, 1982.
History of the Burgh of the Canongate. John Mackay. Johnstone Hunter & Co., 1886.
Memorable Edinburgh Houses. Wilmot Harrison. Oliphant, Anderson & Ferrier, 1898.
The Book of the Old Edinburgh Club, Vol. XXVIII, T.& A. Constable Ltd., 1953.
Edinburgh in the Nineteenth Century, edited W.M. Gilbert, published J. & R. Allan Ltd., 80-86 South Bridge, Edinburgh.

Scott's Fasti 1915, Synod of Lothians & Tweeddale.
New Greyfriars Parish Church. Anon, 1902.
The Scottish Enlightenment. Nicholas Phillipson.
Letters from the Orkney Archives. The Orkney Library, Kirkwall.
Literary and Artistic Landmarks of Edinburgh. Andrew Pennycook, Albyn Press, Edinburgh.
A Tour of Scotland in 1819. Robert Southey. James Thin, Edinburgh.
Robert Burns and Edinburgh. John McVie. Burns Federation, 1969, page 28.
Poetry of Robert Burns. W.E. Henley & R.T. Richardson, Vol. IV, pages 246 & 296; Vol. II pages 224 & 417. Caxton Publishing House, Ltd., Clun House, Surrey Street, London, W.C., 1896.
Sir Walter Scott and His World. David Daiches. The Viking Press, New York, 1971.
Burns, The Man, His Work, The Legend. Maurice Lindsay. McGibbon & Kee 1954, page 194.
Jane Austen's Letters. Edited R.W. Chapman. Oxford Clarendon Press, 1932.
Jane Austen. Douglas Bush, Macmillan Press Ltd., 1975.
Alexander Brunton, Extracts from the Memoir and Life of his wife, affixed to the edition of Mary Brunton's Discipline, Standard Novels No. XVI, published Henry Colburn & Richard Bentley, London; Bell & Bradfute, Edinburgh; Cumming, Dublin; Galignani, Paris.
Walter Scott. The Heart of Midlothian. The Caxton Publishing Co., Clun House, Surrey Street, London, W.C.
Sketches of the Edinburgh Clergy of the Established Church of Scotland. John Anderson, 1832.
Life and Work of Joanna Baillie. Margaret S. Carhart, New Haven; Yale University Press. London; Humphrey Milford, O.U.P., 1923.
Byron - The Years of Fame. Peter Quennell, Reprint Society, 1943.
The Poetical Works of William Cowper. Edited H.S. Milford. O.U.P., 1950.
The 'immortal' who fell from literary grace. Rosalind Russell. The Scotsman, 2 February 1987.
Memorabila Domestica. Rev. Donald Sage. Albyn Press, 1975.
Self-Control, Mary Brunton. Manners and Miller, Edinburgh, 1811.
Famous Scots, The Pride of a Small Nation. Forbes Macgregor. Gordon Wright, Edinburgh, 1984.

CHAPTER VI

Documents in favour of the application of Rev. Alexander Brunton for the Professorship of Oriental Languages, 1812.
Edinburgh in the Nineteenth Century. Edited W.M. Gilbert, published J & R Allan Ltd., 80-86 South Bridge, Edinburgh.
The New Town. Sasha Stevenson. The Visitor, Edinburgh & East of Scotland, 1984.
Mary Brunton's English Journal, 1815. Alexander Brunton's Memoir.

The Warwick Vase. Richard Marks & Brian J.R. Blench, The Burrell Collection, Glasgow Museums & Art Galleries.
Silences that Speak. William Pitcairn Anderson, 54 Hanover Street, Edinburgh, 1931.
Watt & Boulton. Marion C. Robison, Reminiscences of Handsworth, 1972.
James Watt. L.T.C. Rolt, Batsford, 1962.
Discipline. Mary Brunton. Manners & Miller, Edinburgh, 1815.
Letters from Alexander Brunton's Memoir of his wife. Manners & Miller, Edinburgh, 1819.
The Orkney Library Archives, Kirkwall, Orkney.

CHAPTER VII

Letters from Alexander Brunton's Memoir of his wife.
Emmeline, with pieces and extracts from Mary Brunton's correspondence added by Alexander Brunton. Manners & Miller, Edinburgh; Archibald Constable & Co., Edinburgh; John Murray, Albermarle Street, London.
Edinburgh Evening Courant, 28 December 1818.
Edinburgh Advertiser, 29 December 1818.
The Scottish School of Painting. W.D. McKay, R.S.A., Duckworth & Co., London, 1911.

Index

C

H

I

J

K

L

M

N

O

P

U

W